THE

40

QUESTIONS

EVERY WOMAN SHOULD ANSWER

By

Judy M. Langford

This book is a work of non-fiction. Names and places have been changed to protect the privacy of all individuals. The events and situations are true.

ISBN: 1-4140-0633-0 (e-book)
ISBN: 1-4140-0634-9 (Paperback)
ISBN: 1-4140-0635-7 (Dust Jacket)

This book is printed on acid free paper.

1stBooks - rev. 10/23/03

TABLE OF CONTENTS

CHAPTER

INTRODUCTION

Call it a midlife crisis. Call it anything you like, but I have always wanted to write a book. I wanted to write a book that people would read, that they could come away from with a greater sense of self and self worth. More importantly I wanted to write a book that women would read. I decided to write a book for women, about women and by a woman.

I have clung to my dream of writing a book since high school. I was sort of the class poet. I wrote poems about broken hearts. As a teenage girl I considered myself an expert on this matter. Whenever one of my friends got ceremoniously "dumped" I was ready and waiting with a poem. Of course I wrote other types of poetry, but falling in love, unrequited love and love gone wrong seemed to fill most of my pages. I fully intended to publish a book of poetry. I was going to go to college and study Creative Writing. I thought maybe I would write for a newspaper, have a column like my idol, Erma Bombeck. She was the greatest. I remember an assignment in 11th Grade Journalism to write 10 questions you would ask a famous person whom you admire. I chose Erma. I liked her sarcastic wit, and the fact that she wrote as if she were talking. I have probably been influenced by her writing style quite a bit. I wanted to ask Erma the following questions: How does your family feel about being the subject of so many of your books and articles? How does your husband deal with having a famous wife who earns much more than he does? Being a career woman, what is your opinion of the ERA? See, even way back in high school I was asking questions. Somehow in college I got a little sidetracked. I fell in love with a small Catholic college in Loudonville called Siena. They had no creative writing program, so I became an English major. I decided I would be an English teacher. I student taught a religion class and promptly decided teaching was not for me. I would go into Advertising and do Copywriting. I made it to Advertising, landing my first job at BBDO, home of Pepsi, "the best creative department on the street". That's what I always said anyway. I did actually work in the creative department now and then, but as a "floater" doing mostly administrative work. Advertising was long hours and very little pay. I stood that for about a year and a half before deciding to give up the glamour and my ½ days on Fridays (in the summer) for computers on the Paine Webber trading floor. I never looked back. Go figure. Yet I never really let go the idea of writing a book. Over the years I have had several ideas for novels etc…but never actually put "pen to paper" so to speak. I guess the impetus for this book was obvious, turning 40. They say you should write about what you know, and I am getting to know 40. I am getting to know it through the eyes of 15 different women, myself included. I chose the girls that I interviewed based primarily on their age, and the fact that I knew none of them would laugh in my face when told about my aspirations to write a book. You will notice that I constantly refer to them as "girls". I do not care if this is politically incorrect. It is how I think of them, as my "girls". I do not mean this in a derogatory manner. It's just the way I am. Anyway, I thought I should mention that. I think I began with well over twenty women, but a few just weren't interested and a few others just took too long to get their responses back to me (some people still hadn't given me their responses after six months, and I was already writing the book at that point). Though all the women interviewed are between the ages of 38 and 41, all are in different stages in their lives. I have interviewed a few stay-at-home Moms, a few working Moms, and a couple of single, working girls. Two of the women have careers in the military. Some of the women have children, some don't. Some are divorced and some re-married. I think it all makes for some pretty interesting reading. Somewhere in the sea of responses I think most women will find themselves.

In the process of conducting the interviews, I, or I guess I should really say "we" have discovered adjectives for 40 that had never occurred to us before. Forty can be fun, freeing (that word came up a lot in the responses) educating, and liberating, annoying, maturing and just plain frustrating. OK, we have discovered that 40 can indeed be Fabulous.

The process of writing the book was simple some days and complicated on others. I began by concocting "The 40 questions". This number was in fact intentional as was the pun. This in itself took several weeks as I constantly revised the question list. I wanted most of the questions to be thought provoking, but I wanted some to be strictly for fun. I did most of this work in two very strange, and somewhat dangerous places, on my treadmill and in my car. OK, it's a minivan, so sue me. I bought one of those hand held recorders and kept it with me. Ideas would come to me primarily while driving or running because this is my alone time. These are probably the only times of day when my mind is free and clear and I can actually think for a minute and possibly be creative. I really thought I was hot stuff talking into this thing. After I completed "The 40", as I now like to refer to the questions, I had to get up the nerve to ask some of my friends to agree to be interviewed. Who would be my "victims"? (I like to refer to them this way. Again, it's just the way I am. I don't mean anything negative by it). I began with groups of my oldest friends. I have to admit to being a bit disappointed when some of the girls did not want to participate and shrugged it off. I mean here I was trying to live out my dream, to write a book, and they couldn't even muster up a "good luck". I have since decided that that was pretty egocentric of me. This was, after all, my dream, not theirs. Not everyone is comfortable discussing personal things, and some of these questions are very personal. It was really somewhat conceited of me to expect everyone to share my enthusiasm. So I got over it. The women who did participate more than made up for the few who did not. There were even a few women participating who were not on my original "victims" list. I was overjoyed that they liked the concept and were willing to assist me in my endeavor. I received such positive feedback from everyone who participated. Evie and Sophie both told me it was cathartic for them, Ellen had a good time and said it was fun, and so did DeniseB and Tracy. Everyone said it forced her to look at 40 in a new way, a very good way. Anyway, this elevated my spirits and helped move me forward. I thought, "I will write this book". There were many days when I got bogged down by what I thought was a tremendous undertaking and something that would certainly never come to fruition. On these days I just made myself sit down and write. I have been fully aware from the start that this book may never be published, but I decided early on that it will be written, and here it is. This entire process has been a true "labor of love" for me. I am not only referring to writing the book, but to the feeling of completing it with the assistance of 14 wonderful, insightful, non-judgmental, fabulous women.

As I said earlier, I have designed the questions to be mostly introspective and thought provoking. I wanted women to take a good look at their lives, their hopes and dreams, their missed opportunities and their priorities, and then to share them with me. What I did not was for them to obsess or search for the perfect answer. I wanted their first instinct. The first thing to pop into their cluttered minds when posed a question. These first, or "gut responses" are usually the most honest. Most, no all, of the women took much longer to respond and I was concerned they were spending too much time on "how" to answer the questions and not on "what" the answer actually was. Evie was the first to return her responses. Susan was the last. Once I actually sat down to answer the questions myself I realized that they were not that easy to answer. Throw in a couple of kids and or a full-time job, and well, some extra time needed to be taken. So I granted everyone more time than I had originally intended. As I mentioned earlier, I also threw in a handful of just for fun, or "frivolous" questions. Actually these turned out to be just as telling as the more introspective questions. I did this merely to lighten the mood. I believe that Shakespeare referred to this as Comic Relief. After all the responses were received I read through them and I added a few pages of generalizations, summations, notes, what have you, for each question. I added little stories and antic dotes about the victims that were relevant to the particular question. I used our responses and tidbits from our lives as examples. I feel compelled to remind the reader that these are *our* ideas and feelings. Many of the comments are **generalizations** based on the women who participated in the book. I am in no way saying that every woman should agree with or feel the same way as the women here.

I toyed with the idea of breaking the book into chapters, and rearranging the questions, but it just didn't flow well. I decided I should write the book in the exact order of the questions. So I did. I think everyone who reads this book will be pleased to read the responses to question #1 "How do you feel about turning 40"? It sets the tone for the whole book. You must keep in mind that all questions are subject to individual interpretation. I refused to explain the questions to anyone. Two different people read the very same question and come up with two totally different perspectives. For instance on question # 16 "What is your biggest regret in life"? One of the girls was surprised that my answer was not the death of my father when I was 9 years old. While I obviously deeply regret this, I do not feel that there was anything that I could have done to prevent his death. I view the regret question as a more personal one. Something that I either did or did not do. Everyone did not agree with me, and that is a good thing. I feel this is what makes the reading so interesting. We all do not agree.

There are no right or wrong responses here, well, other than say "green" which wouldn't really work as a response to any question. I was ok with a non-response to a question. I just wanted to know why. Was the question just to difficult, too personal, too ridiculous, or did it just not pertain to you? All responses were welcome. I was even willing to accept "Jude, that is none of your damn business"! But no one came up with that! Many people have asked me my favorite question. Now that is a tough one! I liked them all, obviously, because I wrote them. I liked question #36 a lot. "What phrase, cliché, or song lyric best sums up your basic view of life"? That was a fun one, and the answers were great. Some of the lyric choices were so in tune with what we are going through in our lives right now that it is almost as if that song were written just for, let's say, DeniseB (you have to read her response to #36 to find out why).

I have also chosen a "favorite response" to each question and will highlight it after my "summations". I tried to explain why I chose each one as the "favorite". Occasionally, as in question #6 "If you could be anyone, dead or alive, who would it be"? The reason was totally obvious. Susan's response was beautiful, heartwarming and filled with emotion. For many of the other responses that I chose as "favorite" it was just because the answer made me laugh (I believe laughter to be the greatest, most effective drug know to man). There were even a few that, for some reason, just touched me, even though I couldn't quite put my finger on the reason why. And towards the end I copped out on choosing a favorite for one or two of the questions because I just could not *choose!* When I began doing this I never thought it would be so difficult. I tried not to chose my own response as the "favorite", I sort of felt that that was a bit, I don't now, conceited. I think I wound up choosing myself only twice.

The way I have set the book is as follows. I have listed "The 40" meaning the 40 questions first. Before you go on and read everyone's responses you might want to sit down first and answer some or all of the questions yourself. I don't mean that you need to sit down and write detailed, grammatically correct responses. Just go through "The 40" and answer them in your head. Just get a feel for your own responses prior to reading everyone else's. The reason I suggest this is that as I told the girls, your first, gut reaction is probably the most truthful. If you begin by reading the responses of 15 other women you may be affected by their answers and tend to edit your own. Just a thought, all I really ask is that you read it. Sandwiched between "The 40" and the rest of the book is what I call the "biographies". I have included a small paragraph on each of the girls so that you, the reader, can become acquainted with everyone. I think this will make some of their responses easier to understand, and give the reader a more comfortable, intimate, friendly feeling.

So that's it. Sit down, get a glass of wine, put a video in for the kids, put your feet up and read away.

BIOGRAPHIES

Let's begin with a little background on the ladies who participated in the book. I like to jokingly call them my "victims", and you may see them referred to as such later on in the book. These little biographies are designed to assist you while you read their responses and to give you some insight into their answers. Here they are, in the order their responses will appear in the book:

Judy: That's me, the author. Age 39. Married to Michael 14 years. Two boys, Tommy age 8 and Danny 5. I have been mostly a stay-at-home Mom working part-time for a year here and there. I call Motherhood "the toughest job you will ever love". I think this says it all. I worship the ground my parents walk on. My Dad died when I was nine and my mother, Ellie, had the good sense to marry Tom, my father. I don't use the word step. It doesn't apply to us. My brother Donald is 7 years older than I am almost to the day. His birthday is 12/20, mine 12/19. I think I had a good childhood. I was raised in beautiful Rockville Centre, New York. I attended private, catholic college at Siena, in a lovely little town called Loudonville. I made some of the best friends imaginable, many of them consented to be interviewed for this book. It's hard to describe myself. I am a good talker. I don't think anyone would argue with that. I am also a good listener. The two really need to go hand in hand. I am fiercely loyal to my family and circle of friends. I am a mother lion to my children. You can screw with me, but mess with my kids and I will bring the wrath of God down on you. They are my world. I think for a little person I pack a big punch. I love to sware.

Evie: Siena girl and friend since college. Age 39. Evie is a stay-at-home Mom to Cecelia, who is 3 years old. Evie has recently become separated from her husband Chris. In the midst of it all she has remained "grace under fire" as I like to say. She has managed to work through the anger and hurt and put Cecelia's needs first. Evie is strong and she has uncovered her inner strength. She has discovered a love of Yoga and benefited both mentally and physically. I admire her ability to go on. She told me that answering "The 40" was cathartic and made her realize how good things are, in spite of her current situation. Evie comes from a big Irish Catholic family. She grew up in Glen Cove, New York. She has 3 sisters; Susan, Mary and Beth (who is also participating in the interviews) and a brother, Jimmy who is Beth's twin.

Sophie: Age 40. Some of the most inspirational responses I have received. Sophie has been happily married for 10 years and is currently serving in the Military. She has 3 children from a previous marriage. Sophie heard about my project through mutual friends and contacted me to ask if she could participate. I was completely taken back and flattered that a complete stranger would be so willing to assist me and literally pour her heart out. She has truly overcome a life of difficult circumstances and emerged a happy and healthy person. Though I do not know her personally, she sounds like a very strong, grounded and spiritual person.

Ellen: Also a Siena girl. Former roommate. Age 39. Ellen is also a stay-at-home Mom to Connor 7, Griffin 5 and Casey 18 months. Ellen went for the girl. She had more guts than me here so I give her credit for that. Ellen has been married for 9 years to Bob and they live on the Cape where Ellen coaches Field Hockey part-time. Ellen is one of the few people I can talk to about anything. Leo and Marilyn raised Ellen along with her 3 younger brothers, Kevin, Michael and Danny in Glen Head, New York.

Erin: Siena girl, also former roommate. Age 39. Erin is the eternal optimist. She and Frank have been together forever, married 17 years! They have 3 boys, Christopher, David, and Tommy. Erin is the strong silent type. She has endured many health struggles within her immediate family and recently lost her Mom. She made sure to tell her Mom how much she loved her before she passed on. I congratulate her on this. Too many people go through life without doing that. Talking to her you would never know anything was ever amiss in her life. Erin has 3 sisters Lizzie, Vicki and Donna, and two brothers Scott & Philip. They were also raised on Long Island in East Islip. Her brother Philip died, while we were in college, after complications from one of the first heart/lung transplants ever done.

DeniseB: Age 40 and also single! DeniseB is currently working for Financial Technologies International as a Product Manager. She loves to travel (we were travel buddies when I was still single) and has been all over the world. DeniseB has lived in both London and Japan. She has several nieces and nephews that she dotes on. DeniseB has a very sweet disposition except when driving, which I only discovered recently, then she becomes much more aggressive. I loved seeing this side of her! DeniseB was raised in Rockville Centre, New York along with her sisters Michele, Monica, Claudia, MariJean, Paula and her brothers Michael and Patrick.

BethL: Beth is Evie's younger sister. At age 38, she is the baby of this bunch! Beth is recently married to Richard. Beth is a Major and Deputy Surgeon of Medical Operations for Project Enduring Freedom in the US Army. This is a position that can easily put her in harms way, especially since 9/11. As I write this Beth is headed for Afghanistan. Our prayers and our thanks go with her. Beth asked Evie if I thought it would be ok for her to participate in "The 40". I was thrilled that she was interested. Obviously Beth was also raised in Glen Cove, New York, with the same siblings as Evie.

Tracy: Recently turned 40. Tracy is married to Fred for 16 years. Together they have Jennifer 11, Matt 8 and Becky 5. Tracy was also raised in Rockville Centre and is Miss Involved. She is the Treasurer of a Mothers Group and runs the schools Fund Raisers. She played a pivotal role in planning our 20-year high school reunion. People are very comfortable with Tracy. She and Fred recently went through a very difficult time when oldest daughter Jen was diagnosed with LCH and required surgery on her skull. Through it all she remained optimistic and upbeat. Jen is fully recovered and doing very well.

Jenny: Siena girl. Age 39. Single! Jenny recently received her MA in Education with and emphasis on Reading (a personal favorite of mine). She is great with kids and has the patience of a saint. Jenny has a warm and bubbly personality. She is an actor at heart. She performed in many plays in high school and college and she was wonderful to watch. It is always fun to belt out show tunes with Jenny. Her parents, Patrice and Henry raised a their family in Syracuse, New York. Jenny has a sister Maria, and brothers Matthew, Michael and Christopher. She is the ultimate aunt and adores all her nieces and nephews.

Elena: Also age 39, mother of four already with numbers five and six due to come out any minute! Elena has been married to Joe for 12 years. They have 2 boys, Nicholas age 10 and Dillon age 9, and 2 girls, Morgan age 5 and Kendall age 6. Elena is constantly on the go (well obviously). I can't think of a better person to handle six children than Elena. She was an elementary school teacher until the demands of motherhood became too much. Elena loves to sing and has a beautiful voice! I hope one or more of her children inherit this from her. Elena was raised in East Williston, New York by her parents Peggy and Manny and with her sisters Andrea and Cristina and her brother Phillip. Yes, another Siena girl.

Priscilla: Another 39 year old. Priscilla and her husband Lee have been married for over 13 years and have 2 children, Ashlee age 12 and Parker age 11. Priscilla grew up in Simsbury, Connecticut, but spent many summers on the Cape with her Grandmother. After many years as a stay-at-home Mom, she returned to work for Procter and Gamble as an Account Manager in the Pharmaceuticals area. Priscilla is and has always been a fun person to be around. She has a very positive attitude toward life. Priscilla also attended Siena with the rest of us.

BethR: Age 39. Married to Joe forever. Beth is Mrs. Mom. Even my son Tommy was calling her Momma for a while. She has 3 children, Kelsey 11, and the twins, Emily and Jack age 8, born coincidentally on the same day as my Tommy, May 21, 1994. Beth is a Pediatric Nurse by training and I call her all the time for advice. She is an amazing Mom with lots of patience. She is creative and crafty (I hate people with talent). Beth knows way too much about me. I need to keep her close so she doesn't spill any of my dirty little secrets. Fortunately for me I have quite a bit on her too. Beth grew up in Rockville Centre, New York where her parents, Mary and Ron raised Beth along with Bob, Eileen, Rich, Mary and Billy. She attended Villanova University where she met Joe.

Nancy R: Age 39. Nancy and Matt have been married for 11 years and have two boys, Alec, age 9 and Christian age 3. Nancy's Mom, Alicia also lives with them and completes their family unit. Nancy works with my husband at ConvaTec, a subsidiary of Bristol Myers Squibb, in Marketing. Though she was born and raised in the Midwest, she is a New York City girl at heart. I love hanging out with Nancy, we are two "princess in a pod". Nancy and I have had many discussions on how to raise our boys to be good husbands and fathers who love their Mommies!

Susan: Age 39, and one of the single girls. Susan was raised in Dix Hills, New York with her sisters Carolyn and Jennifer and their brother Bill. Susan recently switched careers after leaving Manhattan and IBM for the restaurant business in the Albany area (where many of us attended college at Siena). Though I have not been in touch with Susan much over the years, it doesn't really sound like she has changed much since college. Susan still sounds like the same 'devil may care' girl she was back in our college days. I was so happy that she was willing to participate in the interviews.

DeniseW: Denise was born and raised in New Jersey, she is 41 and has found true love the second time around with husband Alan (who is younger! You go girl). They have been together for two years. Denise has a daughter from her first marriage, Sierra, age 6 who is an absolute pistol. Brittney Spears, look out! Denise works in New York for BBDO, an advertising agency, in New York City (coincidentally where I had my very first job).

Ladies, here are your 40 questions. I want you to take time and think about each one carefully. Please do not try and answer them all at once. You will notice that the questions are somewhat grouped. A handful of introspective questions will be followed by a frivolous question just to lighten things up a bit. Please write down your answers and email them to me at AUTHORJUDY@AOL.COM. If you want to do a few at a time and send me them as you go along, please feel free to do so. I will need your responses ASAP. I do not want you to think about your response for too long or it may become what you think is the right response as opposed to your true feelings. **DO NOT confer with each other on your answers!.** I do not want duplications. There are no right or wrong answers here. I want *your* opinions and *your* feelings. I do not want you to change your answer because you or someone else thought of a better one. That is not the purpose. Go with your first instinct it is usually the most honest. Please be as real and detailed as possible. Please, no one word answers. If on the off chance this actually makes it to publication we can "change the names to protect the innocent" so to speak, though innocent is not the adjective I would choose to describe any of you! If you find any of the questions to difficult or to personal to respond to please write that as your answer.

Thank you for your time and effort. I hope this will be fun for everyone.

1. How do you feel about turning 40? Are you happy, sad, indifferent or angry?
2. Are you the person you expected to be at 40? Are you pretty much where you expected to be at 40?
3. Is 40 better or worse than you thought it would be?
4. How about sex, is it better or worse at 40? Too often or not enough? Did you have a sexual peak, or were you too busy to notice?
5. How has your relationship with your parents and siblings changed from your twenties to now?
6. If you could be anyone else, dead or alive, who would it be? Why?

7. What is the best thing about turning 40? What is the worst?
8. How is your health? What do you do to stay healthy? How have your exercise, eating and skincare habits changed since your twenties?
9. Have you ever lied about your occupation? Why or why not?
10. Have you ever lied about your age? Why or why not?
11. Who has had the biggest influence on your life?
12. What are the characteristics that attracted you to your spouse/significant other? Are they the same or different from the characteristics that you value in them now?
13. If you could be a guest on any TV show which one would it be? Why?
14. Are you prepared for menopause? Have you had any perimenopausal symptoms? How did that make you feel?
15. What is your biggest regret in life?
16. How would you like to be remembered by your family and friends?
17. Are you turning into your mother? Is that good or bad?
18. Do you consider yourself a lucky person? Why or why not?
19. How is your relationship with God? Has this changed since your twenties through early thirties?
20. What actor/musician/politician etc…do you find attractive? What is it about him that you find so appealing?
21. Tell me some things you do just for you? Do you feel guilty about doing them?
22. When was the last time, if ever, you have gone away without your husband/significant other and kids? How did they survive without you? Did you have a good time?
23. Do you think about your own mortality? Has this changed since 9/11? How did 9/11 change you?
24. Are you a good person? Are you a good daughter, wife, mother and employee?
25. What personal event or events in your life have really changed or shaped you?
26. What has changed most about you from age thirty to age 40? Do you view these changes as positive or negative?
27. Are there certain things you feel you cannot wear because you are, or are about to, turn 40? Has your sense of style change much?

28. Ever miss being younger? What age, if any, would you choose to go back to?
29. What do you consider a good day? What little things make you happy?
30. Tell me three attainable goals you want to accomplish in this your 40th year. They must be personal goals. Something just for you.
31. What characteristics do you value in people close to you? What characteristics really rub you the wrong way? Has your core group of friends changed much in the last ten years or so?
32. Did you ever have difficulty turning any of the milestone ages (i.e.: 18, 21, 30, 35) or any age for that matter? How did you get over it?
33. How do you plan (and you shall celebrate) to celebrate the big 40? Or did you crawl in bed and cry?
34. List three adjectives that described you in your twenties through your early thirties. Ok, now list three adjectives that describe you now that you are, or are approaching 40? How do you feel about the changes?
35. Now that you are 40, if someone paid for it, and it was 100% guaranteed safe, would you consider plastic surgery? What would you change? Why?
36. What phrase, cliché or song lyric best sums up you basic view on life?
37. Is there anything missing from your life? Can you do anything to change that?
38. How is today's 40-year-old woman different from when our Mothers were 40? Will it be different for our daughters?
39. Is turning 40 easier for men? Why or why not?
40. What do you hope the next 10 years will bring?

Since a good place to start is the beginning, let's start with Question #1. Enjoy your reading.

CHAPTER 1—HOW DO YOU FEEL ABOUT TURNING 40? ARE YOU HAPPY, SAD, INDIFFERENT OR ANGRY?

Since this question will undoubtedly set the tone for the entire book I was more than pleased to find out that the responses to this question were overwhelmingly positive! Turning 40 distressed hardly anyone interviewed. If you are looking strictly at statistics, of the 15 women who have participated, three cited "indifference" and only two others were able to find some fault with this momentous occasion. Those who cited indifference, Erin, BethR and DeniseB claimed they hadn't really given it much thought. Imagine that! Here they are on the brink of their supposed mid-life crisis and they haven't even given it a second thought. That could work. Only two women, Nancy and Priscilla are even somewhat troubled by the "big 40". Their concerns actually had more to do with how society views them, in their opinion old, then with how they view themselves. I think our generation has been working hard at changing stereotypes that have been around since the beginning of time. One hundred years ago, 40 was old. Life expectancy wasn't much more than that. People married much younger and had children much younger, and might even be, God forbid, a grandparent by their 40th birthday. This is rarely the case anymore. Life expectancy has increased to an average of 76-80 years old. We are now only at the halfway point at 40, and the best is yet to come. I was overjoyed to read that almost everyone was so comfortable with 40. I like it, 40 is a nice round number. It does not sound menacing or threatening to me. I think we all believe that it is what it is, and that is a number. Somewhere along the line someone, probably a man, decided the mere mention of the number 40 should provoke anxiety. It seems this group of women begs to differ. In addition to embracing 40 we are all finding that there is actually a certain wisdom that comes with age. DeniseW found love again recently making turning 40 almost a blessing. Many of us are more comfortable in our own skin than we were in our 20s and 30s. Jenny and Evie say they feel the best they have in a long time. We feel that we know ourselves better mentally and physically, and there is a power that comes with this knowledge. This power is earned. We feel entitled to enjoy our newfound power and wisdom. I cannot stress this enough. Many of us have never experienced these feelings before and we are relishing them. We have become strong, independent women with families and careers that we are proud of. We may have finally "come of age".

I think I enjoyed Ellen's response to this question the best. Let me share it with you. When asked **"How do you feel about turning 40"?** Ellen responded: "In a word happy. If I were to be sad and melancholy about it I think that would prevent me from being excited about the future. So many wonderful things have happened in my life so far that my expectation is that more of the same is waiting for me around the next bend". I just thought that was great. She is looking ahead and anticipating good things. She is actually excited about turning 40. What a great way to start a new decade. A positive outlook can be half the battle. Here's an examples to the contrary. I asked some other friends to take part in the interview process and they declined. The interesting thing here is that some of these people had a rather negative attitude about turning 40. I spoke with one friend on her 40th birthday and her mood was, for lack of a better word, bitchy. Another friend who also declined to be interviewed actually spent her 40th birthday in bed with Haggen Daas. This is bad mentally and physically—what a waste of a day that should have been spent celebrating (you choose the way, for me it will be the spa or shopping) and who needs those Haggen Daas calories!! The third person, who has not yet turned 40, seems to be dreading it. Perhaps, and mind you I do not claim to be Dr. Phil, these women were willing to participate in my interviews because of their positive outlook. What do you think?

Let me share some of the other great responses. After lots of deliberation I decided the order of the responses would be follow the order I received them in. Obviously I received my own responses first, and then Evie's, and so one down the line. Here they are, read and enjoy.

Judy: "I am approaching 40 with a positive attitude. With me it is all about my health. As long as one of my little medical maladies doesn't rear its ugly head that day you will find me at the Spa, the mall and out to lunch (notice the 'and' and not an 'or'). I plan on celebrating. I feel I have earned it".

Evie: "It's funny. When I was in my late 20s I worked with a woman who was almost 40. She looked and felt great. I remember, at that time, I vowed that I too would be 40 and fabulous. When I turned 30 I swore my warranty had run out. My back went out and I messed up my knee skiing. Forty and fabulous became a faint glimmer. Now that I am approaching 40 and going through some major upheaval in my life I have discovered Yoga and rediscovered myself. I am closing in on 40 with a big smile on my face. I feel that I am stronger, physically and emotionally, than I have ever been in my life".

Sophie: "I turned 40 in 2002. I was actually very excited to be 40. I probably feel the best I have felt about myself in my entire life".

Ellen: "In a word happy. If I were to be sad and melancholy about it I think that would prevent me from being excited about the future. So many wonderful things have happened in my life so far that my expectation is more of the same is waiting for me around the next bend".

Erin: "I really haven't given it much thought. I guess I would have to say indifferent".

DeniseB: "Indifferent I guess, I am feeling a little happy and a little sad. I am happy to be turning 40 and to have reached that milestone in my life, but I am a little sad at the thought that my life may now be different".

BethL: "I actually feel pretty good about turning 40. My philosophy has always been, 'as long as you are looking at the grass from the right side, you are ok'. I am currently in a profession that I enjoy and married to a wonderful man.

Tracy: "I am not bothered about turning 40. I am where I think I should be at 40".

Jenny: "I feel good about turning 40—is it because it is still over a year away? I don't think so. It's like my father says 'it beats the alternative'! I feel like I am smarter, more comfortable, and more secure. I know I have accomplished a lot, and that gives me the confidence to know that I can handle whatever comes up. I don't have as many fears and uncertainties as I did when I was in my 20's. And since my body started to betray me around 30, it is not a shock anymore. I know what I have to do to keep myself in shape. Now I have just got to start saving up to have an eye job"!

Elena: "I tend to feel indifferent about turning 40. I think partly because I am still doing the same things that I was doing 10 years ago. I don't feel like 40 is so different than any other age".

Priscilla: "Turning 40 makes me feel a little depressed because the number 40 implies OLD. Also, I can vividly remember being 20 and thinking a 40-year old woman was OLD. Now, of course, I now better! I am also a little excited because it is a time to celebrate. We are all healthy and enjoying our lives at this point and the highlight for my 40th year will be…I am taking my family on a cruise"!

Beth R: "I don't really feel anything about turning 40. I am not sure if that is because it is still a year away, but at this point I am not concerned. It seems like so many of my friends have 'gone before me' so to speak, that by the time I hit 40 it will almost be an afterthought. That is pretty much how I felt about 30 too. Maybe I should answer this question again next year"!

Nancy: "Shocked is the best way to describe how I feel about turning 40 because I do not think of myself as a typical 40 year old woman. I still love to jump around and act like a goofy kid sometimes".

Susan: "How do I feel about turning 40? so hard to answer. I don't think it is hitting me yet. All the other girls (Siena girls) will be turning 40 before me. I have a whole year to watch everyone else turn 40. So by the time it gets to me I will have had some time to sort of get used to the idea. In some ways it is hard to imagine that we are that old. I don't feel that old. So to answer how I feel about it TODAY—I would have to go with 'indifferent'. It is not yet a reality for me. Ask me again this time next year and I will probably be a little unhappy about it. When you are in your 30s you can at least feel like you are still young. But I think 40 may start to put you over the edge".

DeniseW: "When I turned 40 about a year ago I was happy about it. My husband, Alan, made a big deal about it. My birthday is the day after Christmas, and I am usually a bit depressed because the holiday is over, couple that with a birthday and this may not make a happy day. But Alan booked a room in Ocean City Maryland for three nights. It was a great hotel with an ice-skating rink, pool, hot tub, and all the trimmings. We got all bundled up and walked on the boardwalk, had wonderful dinners and drinks. I don't think I ever felt more appreciated or loved in my entire life. It was the way he treated me that made it the best age I ever turned".

CHAPTER 2—ARE YOU THE PERSON YOU EXPECTED TO BE AT 40? ARE YOU PRETTY MUCH WHERE YOU EXPECTED TO BE AT 40?

I have more good news here. I like beginning on such a positive note. It doesn't seem that anyone is disappointed with the person they have become. Not everyone is who or what she expected to be at 40, but we have discovered, as in my own case that this is not necessarily a bad thing. In my 20s I fully expected to be VP at Barclays Bank. That was my goal. I was not going to even consider children until I was 35 (which almost happened, much to my dismay). I had big career goals and I wanted big money and a nice title. I enjoyed working. I loved being in New York. There is no place like it. Children just seemed like a lifetime away. Enter reality, or rather fertility problems. Enter complete and total change of life priorities. At 39 I am a stay-at-home Mom who has only worked part-time over the last 8 years. I would not have it any other way. I do not ever, not for one second regret my decision. Which is not to say that I do not miss working, I do. I miss using my brain, I miss the social interaction, I miss accomplishing a task, I miss NY and I miss my paycheck and my bonus. I also miss reviews. I would love for someone to sit me down once a year and say "Judy, let's see, you've been at the Mommy level for 8 years now. We feel you are doing very well in communication, raising good boys and general housewifery. You strong suits are disciple and affection. Nice balance here. Congratulations. We do feel that you may need a little more work in the patience area, especially the yelling. Maybe take it down a notch. We figure a 6% raise this year with your usual 20% bonus will keep you happy. Keep up the good work. You are a valuable member of our team". Now, how great would that be? So even though I am nowhere near what I expected to be, I do believe I am exactly where I am supposed to be. For this I am ever thankful.

For some of us life dealt us a hand and we had to work with what we have. We try to make the best out of bad situations, change what we can and live with what cannot be fixed. Some of us have not reached the goals we set up for ourselves many years ago, but I notice we have not stopped trying to achieve them. BethL expected to be a mom by now, but still sees that in her future and works toward it. Until this becomes a reality for her she is enjoying her career as one of our ladies in uniform, serving as a Major in The United States Army. Jenny has recently received her MA in Education and is finally working in the field she has always wanted to be in. Sophie notes that there was a time when she wasn't even capable of looking ahead let alone thinking about who and where she might be at 40. Now that she has finally arrived at 40 she is happy to be there. This is all fabulous news. If you are not the person you expected to be or are not satisfied with the person you are I hope you can see here that 40 is not too old to change. As a matter of fact I think it is a good age to assess and regroup. Figure out why you are not "who" you expected to be. This is no easy task, but the process itself can be enlightening.

I think you will find my favorite answer to question # 2 a surprise. I know the wonderful woman whose answer it is will be shocked that I chose her response as my favorite answer to #2. I adored Beth R.'s answer. It warmed my heart, and I was so thrilled to hear that women still feel this way and are proud to admit it.

When asked, "Are you the person you expected to be at 40? Are you pretty much where you expected to be at 40"?

Beth's response was, "I don't really think I 'expected' to be anything at 40. I know that I 'expected' to feel older and more 'grown up' than I do. I basically still feel like a 20 year old in an almost 40 year old body. I never had any big career aspirations because that wasn't the vocation I chose for myself. I always envisioned myself being a Mom and being home with my children—which is exactly where I am now".

I ask you, is this not the ultimate answer? Beth R. is doing EXACTLY what she planned. How many people, men or women, do you know who could say this? I would like to add that Beth R. is also doing an amazing job. I know her children and they are wonderful, smart, polite, happy, well adjusted and beautiful. We have even thrown around the idea of my oldest son Tommy marrying her daughter Emily. Since they happen to share a birthday, we figure this will be one less date for him to forget. Bravo to Beth.

Here are the remaining answers:

Judy: "Definitely not, but this is not a bad thing. I am very happy with where I am in my life. In my 20's I thought at 40 I would be a VP at Barclays Bank and a full-time working Mom. I never thought I would be a stay-at-home Mom. I was very career-oriented back then. I actually still am, only my career has changed. I am now a career Mom. I am thankful I had a choice. For me it was a no brainer. This is where I was meant to be".

Evie: "Yes in some ways, no in others. I expected to be fabulous and feel good about myself and I am working on that part. I also expected to be happily married with a couple of children and that has all changed. Instead, I am a separated single Mom with one beautiful, intelligent, wondrous daughter, Cecelia. And that is OK. Not what I expected, but certainly OK".

Judy M. Langford

Sophie: "I guess I never really planned this far ahead. Over the years I have had recurrent problems with depression and actually never looked to be 40. But, since I am in good health and found a marriage partner who completes me, I have become excited about who and where I am".

Ellen: "Honestly, I do not know what I expected to be or where I expected to be at 40. But, put on the spot I would have to say 'yes', I always expected to be married with children and I am. I guess I thought I would feel older, but I really don't".

Erin: "I don't think I had any particular expectations. I try to live each day and each year for the opportunities and challenges it presents".

DeniseB: "I am the person I expected to be, however, not where I thought I would be".

BethL: "I actually thought I would be a full-time Mother by now. Seeing as I am 38, I still plan on reaching that goal. My career has changed considerably. I went from working at a huge Health Care system on Long Island to being back full-time in the US Army".

Tracy: "Yes, I am who I expected to be and where I expected to be".

Jenny: "Since I am not there yet, it is hard to say. In my experience, life is like a meanderings river, lots of twists and turns, so in many ways things are different than I thought, but in other ways they remain the same. Like my career—I always thought I would be a teacher eventually. I wanted to do other things too - and that's how it turned out. As far as the person I expected to be—who I am, what I stand for, what my values are—yes, for the most part, I am that person".

Elena: "I think that I am what I had hoped for at 40. My life could have gone so many different ways, career, marriage etc…But as a person, intellectually and spiritually I think I am pretty much who I hoped I would be".

Priscilla: "Honestly, I never gave this much thought. I was enjoying my life at the time and never really imagined myself as an older person. If I look back though, I guess I am in a better place than I really thought I would be, because, once again, I thought of a 40 year old as an OLD person".

BethR: "I don't really think I 'expected' to be anything at 40. I know that I 'expected' to feel older and more 'grown up' than I do. I basically still feel like a 20 year old in an almost 40 year old body. I never had any big career aspirations because that wasn't the vocation I chose for myself. I always envisioned myself being a Mom and being home with my children—which is exactly where I am now".

Nancy: "I think I am much better than I ever thought I would be at 40. I feel younger and have taken on a more carefree spirit than when I was younger. I seem to be enjoying life more now and not taking things for granted. Believe it or not, having young children at an older age has made me feel young again. I run and dance around with my two children and see the world through their innocent eyes".

Susan: "Am I the person I expected to be at 40? Am I where I expected to be? I don't know what I expected to be at 40. I don't think I ever gave it much thought before. It always seemed so far away. I guess if you had asked me back in college, I would have thought I would be married with kids by the time 40 rolled around. But I am not. Well, I still have almost a year, so I guess I shouldn't totally rule that out! But I am happy. I have my health and I have a good family, with nieces and nephews that I adore. I have friends that I made in college, and prior, who are still as close as ever. And I have new friends I have made over the years. I have had relationships that were good, and some that were not so good. All in all, I can't complain about the life I have led. If I am not where I expected to be, that is ok. Everything I have done over the years has moved me on my way to who and what I am now. Hope that answers your question". Yes Susan, it answers the question very nicely.

DeniseW: "I am much more successful career wise than I thought I would be. As far as 'the person' I was meant to be, I don't think I actually 'found myself' until I was just about 40, so I really didn't have any expectations".

CHAPTER 3—IS 40 BETTER OR WORSE THAN YOU THOUGH IT WOULD BE?

Since most of us have not actually reached 40 yet (at the time this was written only Sophie, DeniseB, Tracy and DeniseW are 40) actually a lot of this is conjecture on our parts. As one friend told me on her 40th birthday, "you can walk the walk and talk the talk, but on December 19th it will all change". December 19th just happens to be my 40th birthday, and she was referring to my decidedly optimistic attitude which she is sure will change on 12/19/02. The ladies interviewed, and I, beg to differ. It seems to me that I have either found the 15 most optimistic, self-assured, enthusiastic women in the world, or women in general are changing their attitudes about turning 40. During our mothers' reign, turning 40 meant an end of youth, and end to fun, even and end to our childbearing years. This is just no longer the case. Today's 40-year-old woman, at least as I see it, is something more like this. There is a career, which can be as a homemaker and Mom or out in the business world. She generally takes good care of herself. She likes to stay fit by working out, eating right and moisturizing (we do this a lot). She pursues some outside interest to get a much-needed break from her busy career as Mom,

Lawyer, Accountant, Teacher or what have you. She is strong-willed and opinionated and somewhere in the last few years she has come to realize that this is a good thing. She is no one's doormat. She sounds pretty terrific to me.

Some of us had no idea what to expect when turning 40. In a way this is a good thing. Our mothers, and countless other women either directly or indirectly involved in the sexual revolution and the women's movement of the 60's and 70's gave us a huge gift. They gave us choice, and the freedom to enjoy those choices. And guess what? It appears we are! We have them to thank for the overwhelmingly positive response to this question. Almost everyone interviewed said 40 was "better" than they expected. We look better, we feel better, and we are better. Sophie cited trouble with physical changes and some difficulty with unattained goals. But I ask you; do you know anyone who has achieved all their life goals by their 40th birthday? If you had, what would you dream about, what would you aspire to? Time isn't running out as Sophie feared, it's just time to get moving.

My favorite response was Jenny's. I loved every word of it. It rings completely true. I think many women will read this response and shake their heads as if saying "yes, yes, me too"! See if you are one of them. When asked ***"Is 40 better or worse than you thought it would be"?*** Jenny's answer was: "I think it will be better. When we were kids, remember what 40 was? It was old, and not because that was our perspective as children. I think that was the prevailing American Attitude. Forty is much younger, much more positive, much more powerful, and much more vital than it used to be, because people in this generation have refused to think of 40 as a big deal. I think it is a big deal, but in a good way—it's great to get older. I remember when my mother turned 50 she said 'I am glad that I am 50 because now I am going to do what I want and not take any crap from anyone anymore'! (Which wasn't terribly different from the way she was before). But she meant that she had the freedom backed up with the knowledge. When you are young, you're free and strong, but you get pushed around more. There really is wisdom that comes to you as you age, and that is empowering. So I took a page from my mother's book and started using her philosophy years ago. I'll say 'you can't push me around. I'm 38.'"

Let's take a look at the other responses to Question #3. It is worth noting that not one response included the word "worse".

Judy: "I never really thought much about 40 until this year. I think 40 can be great. I pretty much think it will be what I choose to make of it. I hope to make it good".

Evie: "Well, I haven't quite hit it yet, but compared to my mid-to-late thirties, I am actually looking forward to it. Pretty strange huh?

Sophie: "40 is harder than I thought for two reasons. First, my physical changes, due to aging, make me look more critically at myself, yet I still don't feel the need for anything drastic like plastic surgery. I need to feel better in my own skin. Second, I feel failure more acutely: missing out on a promotion, not finishing school, things of that nature. I guess I see the time in which to complete my goals as shorter".

Ellen: "Better. I feel better physically, and am a little more secure with myself. And my husband can afford me".

Erin: "Probably better. When I was younger I always thought 40 was so old. Now I don't think that at all"!

DeniseB: "I think it is better. I think it is a milestone that I am happy to have reached. In a way it is easier to be single, as you get older. I am happy with my life even though there are some things that I wish were different".

BethL: "40 I hope will be much better. I still think that twenty-seven is the ultimate age. You are still young enough to do just about anything with little or no sleep. You have been on your own for a while and are supporting yourself. As I approach 40 I find the need for more sleep very annoying. I don't want to miss anything".

15

Tracy: "I think it will be better. Forty seemed so old when I was in my 20's, but now it is not old at all. I am married, have 3 children, a dog and a mortgage. For me that is what 40 should be".

Jenny: "I think it will be better. When we were kids, remember what 40 was? It was old!! And not just because that was our perspective, but because we were children. I think that was the prevailing American Attitude. Forty is much younger, much more positive, much more powerful, and much more vital than it used to be, because people in this generation have refused to think of 40 as a big deal. I think it is a big deal, but in a good way—it's great to get older. I remember when my mother turned 50 she said 'I am glad that I am 50 because now I am going to do what I want and not take any crap from anyone anymore'! (Which wasn't terribly different from the way she was before). But she meant that she had the freedom backed up with the knowledge. When you are young, you're free and strong, but you get pushed around more. There really is wisdom that comes to you as you age, and that is empowering. So I took a page from my mother's book and started using her philosophy years ago. I'll say 'you can't push me around. I'm 38'".

Elena: "I don't feel any older or any different than I felt 10 years ago".

Priscilla: "I'll let you know next year! I still have a few months left. I do expect it to be BETTER because I now feel that 40 is NOT old, even if I did believe that at 22".

Beth R: "I guess 40 is better than I thought it would be especially since I don't even feel 40".

Nancy: "Forty is definitely much better than I ever envisioned it would be. I thought I would be sitting in my rocking chair on the front porch watching the world go by. Yet here I am at 40 and I still very much want to be the one in the middle of all the fun".

Susan: "Is 40 better or worse than I expected? I will let you know when I get there"!

DeniseW: "Outside of trying to have a child and age being a factor here, 40 is better than I expected it to be".

CHAPTER 4—HOW ABOUT SEX, IS IT BETTER OR WORSE AT 40? TOO OFTEN OR NOT ENOUGH? DID YOU HAVE A SEXUAL PEAK, OR WERE YOU TOO BUSY TO NOTICE?

Sex, sex, sex. This has to be one of the most debated topics ever. Men and women never seem to agree here. Too much, too little, when, where, how, with whom? Americans are obsessed with sex. If you look at the cover of ANY magazine you will find at least one lead story about sex. "How to have better, multiple orgasms" "Ten ways to drive your lover mad with desire" "Sex in public, good or bad"? The remainder of the articles will probably be about losing weight. Let's face it, sex sells. The more sex, the better something sells. Maybe if I say sex enough, this book will sell. Anyway, I liked this question. I actually liked it a lot. It seems we are a pretty sexy bunch. Our husbands may not agree, but that's a man thing. They never get enough.

As women, we were supposed to have a sexual peak somewhere around the age of 35. Men on the other hand have theirs at around 17 years old. Hello, Mrs. Robinson. Who came up with this? Are we all supposed to have affairs with 17-year old boys? Why would we want to? What would our husbands think? Here's what I think. Men live most of their lives in their sexual peak, so whenever we get to ours is considered good timing for them. Some of us, like Erin, feel they had their peak when they were young, early 20's. This actually makes more sense to me. In your early 20's you are, for starters young. This alone implies energy and a certain carefree attitude toward almost everything, especially sex. You are also without many of the responsibilities that come with age, i.e.: kids. Kids kill your sex life. Don't let anyone tell you differently. Every women I know who has had a baby has lied about the amount of time needed to pass before she may become sexually active again. Let's face it childbirth is the ultimate turn-off. Since most of us are having babies in our late 20 and early-mid 30's, this doesn't seem to be a good time for a "peak" either. Seems to me that 40 could be a good time for a sexual peak. I mean, why not? At this point we are the confident, competent, sexy women we have been striving to be since we turned 18. DeniseW feels that in fact her peak may have occurred in her late 30s and is still going strong. Most of us cited that feeling better about ourselves helps us feel sexier. Ellen, BethR., BethL and I feel very comfortable with our spouses. We can now communicate what it is that we need and want. What makes us feel good and what doesn't work for us. We also know a bit more about how to please our mate. We are even getting more adventurous as we get older. In conversations that I have had with several of these women (for their children's sake I won't name names) I know that recently they have been trying new things and new places to have sex. There is the mini-van and the shower, the coffee table and the staircase, the closet and the pool. Seems like we are more daring now then when we were younger! This all makes for a better sexual experience for both parties, don't you think?

Not everyone is on the same page here sexually, so to speak. Evie, Susan and DeniseB, who are all single right now, are not involved in sexual relationships. And DeniseB says she was too busy building a career to notice if she did have a sexual peak. I actually liked Evie's response to this question even though it wasn't the response I was looking for. When posed the *question **"How about sex, is it better or worse at 40? Too often or not enough? Did you have a sexual peak, or were you too busy to notice"?*** This is her answer, in true Evie style: "Huh? Sex? Oh yeah, I remember that. At this point it doesn't really apply to me unfortunately". I like that Evie poked fun at it.

Here are the remaining responses:

Judy: "Sex is definitely better. I am more comfortable with sex and with myself. I think I am more adventurous. We have more sex now than ever (though my husband would beg to differ). I definitely enjoy it more. Fertility problems put a real damper on sex for me for a long time. You have to have sex at a specific time and day, drugs and tests are involved, romance is not. It really took me a long time to just enjoy sex for the sake of sex again. I had my peak at about 34-35. I think we both enjoyed it".

Evie: "Huh? Sex? Oh yeah, I remember that. At this point it doesn't really apply to me unfortunately".

Sophie: "Sex has gotten better as I have gotten older. I have slowed some due to a medication side effect, but I find sex much more satisfying now. I know now to ask for what I want and know how to please myself when I don't get it. I don't think I need it as much but I do find it to be a very enjoyable perk to marriage".

Ellen: "Better than when I was younger because we are more comfortable with each other and doing different things to find pleasure. However, we do not have sex often. I definitely do not know if I had a sexual peak. If you are referring to just frequency, I would have to say my peak was in my early 20's and early 30's".

Erin: "Sex is still wonderful, but different. I think it goes through different stages, just as my marriage has. If you asked Frank, I know he would definitely say "not enough sex". As for me, I think it is just right. I definitely had a peak early in our relationship or was it just that we were so young and had so much time for each other".

DeniseB: "Sex—not enough. If I had a peak I was too busy to notice".

BethL: "Sex is great. When my husband and I are in the same state, we keep each other very satisfied. We have yet to turn each other down. Not having children probably helps the opportunity factor quite a bit. I don't think I have reached my sexual peak yet, either that or I have been there for years".

Tracy: "Sex is better at 40 because I know what I like and I am not intimidated to ask for it. I do not have the same sex drive however, and could do it less than we do. When we are alone or on vacation though, my sex drive increases because I only have me to worry about and not the kids. I hope I didn't have a sexual peak and miss it"!

Jenny: "Never is not enough, right"?

Elena: "Sex itself is great. Attitude towards is what has changed for me. I don't believe it is my age that has changed my attitude; I think it is my life. If I were single or married without kids I wonder if I would feel differently. Because of family and my busy lifestyle I find I don't crave sex itself. It seems like one more thing someone needs me for. I crave the intimacy more now".

Priscilla: "Sex is great, very comfortable, and I have it often enough, my husband would tell you we don't have it enough! Not sure about a sexual peak. Hey, maybe I didn't have mine yet"!

BethR: "I really thought about this one for you and I would say my peak was about 34ish. In reality I feel there are many little peaks and valleys for me that are constantly changing. Phases that come and go without any real reason, and of course phases that come and go for obvious reasons i.e.: busy days when I go to bed exhausted are always valleys, and happy, not so busy times, especially vacations (but not at my parents house) tend to be my peaks. I figure if I Joe and I could ever get away without the kids we could probably get to a whole new level! As per your question of better or worse, I would have to say more predictable and more "to the point" would be how I describe it—so depending on your mood and time frame that can definitely be better, but can also be worse".

Nancy: "Sex? What's that? Sex, or the lack of it, has nothing to do with my age. It has everything to do with always having a little munchkin between my husband and I in bed, or with not sleeping in the same room with my husband. We seem to play musical bedrooms, on any give night one of us falls asleep in one of the boy's rooms, the sunroom, the guest room or the basement. You figure it out".

Susan: "Sex at 40? Well since I am not currently in a relationship and therefore not having any sex I would have to say I am not getting it enough! Actually, I am not getting it at all. If I go back to my last relationship (@2years ago) I would still say not enough. I manage a restaurant and have a schedule that consists of late nights, early mornings and double shifts. My partner also worked in the restaurant business. With our schedules being what they were, there was hardly even any time to be together, let alone have sex. It is not easy to have a relationship in this business. It is not that I don't meet men. I meet plenty of them. But who wants to date some guy who comes into the restaurant every night to get loaded? Not exactly what I am looking for".

DeniseW: "Well, if I peaked it was in my late 30's and it is still continuing. I do not know if it was an actual peak, or that I just met the right man. If it was both it has been great timing and has continued for over four years. Yippee"!

CHAPTER 5—HOW HAS YOUR RELATIONSHIP WITH YOUR PARENTS AND SIBLINGS CHANGED FROM YOUR TWENTIES UNTIL NOW?

If there is one thing I have learned over the course of my ALMOST 40 years, it is that relationships are forever changing. What makes our relationships with our immediate family so fascinating is that these people may be the only people who have known us for our entire lives. We begin our lives as totally dependent infants. A baby relies completely on the love, affection and nurturing of his/her parents or caregivers. We stay pretty much dependent little beings until we are old enough to go away to college or move out of our parent's homes. During the years in-between we go through various stages in the evolution of our relationships with parents and siblings. Our siblings seem more willing to let us age, perhaps this is because they are going through the same changes and are hoping that we will respect them in the same way. Our parents are a different story. Most of us mention that our parents really did not treat us like adults until we made them Grandparents. As if having a baby of our own makes us an adult. Personally, and help me out here, I have never felt more helpless and in need of my parents than after my first child was born. I just wanted my Mommy there. I still do. I am happy to report that several of us feel that we have always had a good relationship with our parents, especially our mothers, and that this has only improved with time. Almost all of us mention that we have a new and better understanding for and about our parents as we have matured. We actually seek out their advice. Sometimes we even follow it. We even find ourselves using the very same phrases and clichés our parent drove us mad with when we were younger. I ask you, and be truthful, how many of you have said "because I am the mother, that's why"! Perhaps we realize just how difficult it is being an adult. Or perhaps as Susan says we just have more in common now. Perhaps we have come up in age and they have mellowed a bit. Whatever the reason, it seems to be working out for everyone here.

Some of the "victims", especially those from large families, say that their relationships with their siblings have changed drastically. Brothers and or sisters that were once a major annoyance, a tag along, and a tattletale have now become friends. In Jenny and Evie's cases, sisters can be especially close. The intimacy level here is unique and special and should be revered. Most men do not attain friendships like this, especially with a sibling, so it is hard for them to comprehend how two women can spend a whole day together and still need to talk on the phone for an hour and a half the very next day. Jenny refers to this phenomenon as "the sister thing" and her poor brother-in-law just doesn't get it. It seems like we are able to appreciate and accept our siblings and even enjoy their company. One of the greatest things about siblings is that they give us nieces and nephews.

I was just actually scrolling through the pages here; I go back and forth with the writing of this book. I am pretty much doing it in order of the questions, but sometimes I skip around because I am in a mood. So today I am looking a the responses to question #5 about siblings and family and I can't help but notice everyone had A LOT to say here! We had as much to say about our relationship with our parents and sibling as we did about our sex lives. Pretty interesting don't you think?????

I think the award for favorite response goes to Erin here. Read it first and then I will tell you why I chose hers. When asked, *"**Has your relationship with your parents and siblings changed from your twenties until now"?**" Erin responded: "My relationship with my Mom had changed over the last couple of years. My Mom died in February 2002. I think knowing her days were limited made me open up to her in a way that I might not have before. I told her openly over the past couple of years how much I loved her, something that I hadn't done before (this was just not the way in our family). I asked her questions and found out things about her childhood. It was a very positive experience. With my Dad, brother Scott and sisters Linda, Vicki and Lizzie, things have pretty much remained the same. I love them all and enjoy being with them but we don't get together too often because of where everyone lives. Linda did move to Richmond last year and that has been wonderful. I think we had been apart for some 16 years and forgotten how much fun growing up and being together is".

I think it is so important to tell people we love them. And then tell them again and again. I love that Erin asked her Mom questions and was interested in finding out about her Mom's childhood. I am sure her Mom loved this too. I am also happy for Erin that she will not have to live with the feeling of never telling a loved one how you feel. Now everyone go call someone you love and tell them you love them. That is an order!

The rest of us feel this way about the tangled web of family relations:

Judy: "My relationship with my parents has always been very good, I would even dare to say excellent. I literally worship the ground they walk on. I can honestly say the feeling is returned. The three of us know what it is like to has loved and lost. My Dad died when I was nine and Tom was divorced before he met my Mom. I think we all really appreciate finding each other. I have always been able to talk to them and enjoy their company. Sometimes I even take their advice! Which is not to say they don't occasionally drive me nuts, because they do. That's what parents are for isn't it? I mean I know I make my kids nuts sometimes. Hey, I learned from the master. In all seriousness I would not trade them for the world. My brother is 7 years older than I am and was married with 3 kids before I even graduated college. They are all adults now and he is single so we seem to be forever on different pages of our lives, but actually it has always been like this so our relationship has not really changed much over the years".

Evie: "My family has always been close. I am 1 of 5 children; my daughter Cecelia is one of 10 grandchildren. We have grown larger and closer over the years. What is interesting is how your relationship with your parents changes after you have children. You become aware of just how deeply they love you because you now feel that same love for your child. You finally truly appreciate the sacrifices they have made".

Sophie: "We, my family, had a very difficult break. My Mom found it difficult to let us go. Now I make an active attempt to attend special events, although my other siblings do not. My Mom has eased up a bit. With my father there were issues of sexual abuse. This has been dealt with and he and I have a cordial relationship. My folks are still married".

Ellen: "My relationship with my family has improved. Being the only girl with 3 brothers I never enjoyed the same closeness the boys shared. Therefore my relationship with my parents has always been the close one. It has gotten better with my mother over the years and remained the same with my Dad who I have always been close with". (Ellen and I were roommates our first year at Siena. On our very first night together we talked about our families and we both described ourselves as Daddy's girls. I guess some things never change)

Erin: "My relationship with my Mom had changed over the last couple of years. My Mom died in February 2002. I think knowing her days were limited made me open up to her in a way that I might not have before. I told her openly over the past couple of years how much I loved her, something that I hadn't done before (this was just not the way in our family). I asked her questions and found out things about her childhood. It was a very positive experience. With my Dad, brother Scott and sisters Linda, Vicki and Lizzie, things have pretty much remained the same. I love them all and enjoy being with them but we don't get together too often because of where everyone lives. Linda did move to Richmond last year and that has been wonderful. I think we had been apart for some 16 years and forgotten how much fun growing up and being together is".

DeniseB: "Relationship with my family has gotten closer".

BethL: "My Mother actually treats me like an adult. I have a husband and a house, so I guess I qualify. My Dad has treated my like an adult since I graduated college and started earning my own way. I have always had a great relationship with my siblings. We are close in age and grew up together. My lifestyle in the military keeps them worried, but other than that, they are my dearest friends. All of my siblings are parents which leaves me out of certain conversations about the kids".

Tracy: "Regardless of our ages, we are all adults now and the same. I think we have gotten closer".

Jenny: "Like most other things I think it has gotten stronger. I have always been close to my family, but one thing I have really enjoyed, as I have gotten older is how our relationship has deepened and matured. We really enjoy each other as adults. It is a constant source of wonder to me that how my brothers, who were so often annoying to me as children are now such nice guys. Of course, that is a bit of an exaggeration, because of course I always loved them, and there were plenty of times we got along and enjoyed each other when we were kids, but we have so much fun now. It's not like that with my sister. Since she's my only sister, we have always been close, and I always know we would continue to be close. Sometimes her husband says to her 'you were on the phone with your sister for an hour and a half. What were you talking about? You just spent the whole day with her'! Poor guy, he just doesn't get it-it's a sister thing. As for my parents, I have just gotten to know them and appreciate them more—and of course, as adults, we all see things from their perspective now. Sadly, all these benefits come with a dark side. Now, I not only think all my father's corny jokes he told ad nauseam in my childhood are funny, but I am telling them to my nieces and nephews. And I take the same joy in watching them cringe that my dad did with us".

Elena: "I no longer seek their approval only their advice. I think the age gap between parents and also between my siblings and I has disappeared. We now treat one another as equals".

Priscilla: "Actually my relationship with my Mother (my Dad died when I was 23) is fine although we live far apart. I hope, as she ages, that this does not become a problem. I would like to be able to help her more often than I am able to now due to the distance. Siblings are fine too. We have a blast when we get together because our children also have fun when we all get together. My sister has become a bit snobby and thus we do not share a lot. I wish we were closer, emotionally and physically".

BethR: "I think my relationship with my Dad has been changing a lot since my Mom died. 1. I feel more like a 'caretaker' not so much literally, but in the way I feel about him—you know—more protective and concerned about him. 2. My Dad and I really talk more. Before my Mom passed away I would bring things up to her for discussion and spent the bulk of our visits with her. Now he is beginning to fill this role too. 3. My Dad also comes to me with more 'stuff' now. He asks my opinion and wants to talk more than ever before. Maybe he is a little lonely".

My relationship with my siblings hasn't changed much except that now there is a lot more of them! Some I talk to more and are closer to, my sisters, Mary and Eileen. Rich is the only one who has fallen more out of my life. I do think part of the reason is distance, but we also just have less in common now. I am closest with Billy and Donna and I think that is just because we enjoy each others company a lot."

Nancy: "My Mom lives with us now which is awesome. She is such a huge help and a comfort to all of us and she is able to be an integral part of my sons' lives. This situation may not be for everyone, but it works out really well for us. We're more like sisters now—we talk about clothes and jewelry, all that fun stuff".

Susan: "Relationships with parents and siblings definitely gets better as you get older. When you are in your 20s, especially the early 20's you are still a child in the eyes of your parents. As an adult you can now relate on a different level. You can talk about things you couldn't before. You can be more of a friend. My Dad died 10 years ago. My Mother and I have definitely grown closer. I have taken vacations with her and we had a good time. She still has the power to drive me nuts though. While I may be an adult with my own life, I am still her child and she still feels like she can tell me what she thinks is best for me, or wrong with my life etc…However, now I can tell her it's my life and my decisions and she will respect that, under protest of course. I am also closer with my sisters and brother. We used to fight over stupid stuff all the time when we were younger. My sister would wear my clothes without asking, my brother would tell me whom I could and couldn't talk to—really stupid stuff. But now we talk on the phone and discuss our problems, share feelings and help each other out. You get older and you see what is truly important. It is important to have a good relationship with your family. While some friends may come and go, your family will always be there for you, no matter what".

DeniseW: "In my 20's I was still into partying so I don't think I put a lot of emphasis on this. I went through a really bad time, a divorce from my first husband, in my mid-30's and that's when I saw the true colors of members of my 'family'. To make a long story short, I have an ok relationship with my mother and we are working to improve it. I have a strained relationship with one of my sisters and my father. I wish to keep it that way".

CHAPTER 6—IF YOU COULD BE ANYONE, DEAD OR ALIVE, WHO WOULD IT BE? WHY?

Well, we have finally made it to one of the fun questions. I had to do something to liven things up a bit. Since we cannot, or I should say should not live our lives without a little merriment, this question, and the other 4 "fun" questions are designed to give us just that. But it seems that most people, myself included, took the question quite seriously! I was actually amazed at the responses. I guess I expected most answers to be more like Erin and Evie's. They both picked famous people. Erin went to the humanitarian route, choosing Mother Teresa. Erin admires Mother Teresa's selflessness and kindness. She aspires to be more like her. My only concern here is that Mother Teresa had one difficult life. But I guess that is part of what makes her such a great humanitarian.   To be able to put others first, sacrificing everything. I say "Bravo" to Erin. This is a truly wonderful, inspirational choice. Evie on the other hand went with what I might call the "fantasy" response. Evie couldn't decide between Diane Chambers of "Cheers" fame and being a Nurse on ER. I love that these are fictional people. That is part of the fun of all these questions; everyone interprets them in their own way. For Evie, the passionate love, hate relationship between Sam and Diane was appealing, and as far as being a Nurse on ER, it was the Dr. Carter connection that won her over. Erin and Evie had two very different answers, but I thought they were both great.

What really surprised me were Sophie, DeniseW, Tracy and Beth R's responses. Like me, they all chose to remain themselves. BethR actually scares me a bit. Several of our answers were so similar. We both feel that every person no matter how rich, famous, beautiful, intelligent or seemingly perfect carries with them their own special baggage. BethR and I also feel that many people keep this "baggage" hidden from the rest of the world in order to present that "perfect" façade. We don't all walk around with our hearts on our sleeves and maybe this is best. Tracy got right to the point simply stating, "I would be me". DeniseW echoes almost the same exact sentiment. Sophie also feels that she has worked hard to be who she is right now and she is proud of that. I really love that some people other than myself would choose to remain themselves. I think it really shows that we 40 and almost 40 year olds think we have done a pretty good job raising ourselves. I also think that if we had asked this question several years ago that more of the responses would be to be other people. Again, I think a lot has to do with the grace and contentment that only comes with age and experience. Before you all start to blow off steam at me, let me just say I do not think choosing to be someone else is wrong, or even less right. Especially if you pick Mother Teresa, my God! I think if you had asked me this question when I was going through fertility problems I definitely would have picked someone like Carol Brady. Three boys, three girls, perfect family. I am just in a totally different place now. This is not to say that we don't occasionally envy other people. BethR admits to having moments of "it must be great to be so and so". I think we all do that at one time or another. I think this is normal as long as it is kept down to just that, moments.

For some of the questions I have a tough time choosing a favorite response. All the answers are great. I had no problem choosing a favorite response for this question. My favorite response is Susan's. It is just beautiful, and a testament to family (even that 'sister thing' again). I think her sister Carolyn will be very happy and proud when she reads Susan's response. Susan sent me her responses in groups, starting with questions 1-10. She noted next to question #6 that she would have to get back to me, that this was a thinker. A few hours later I received this email, which I will print in its entirety. Be prepared, this one comes with a 10-hanky warning.

"Hi again. I sent out my responses to you, turned off the computer and hopped in the shower. I'm in the shower trying to remember what the question was that I said I would get back to you on when I realized it was the one about who would you like to be, dead or alive. So I am thinking about this and I am trying to think of some inspirational people and why they would be someone I would like to be. Then it hits me. I have the answer to that question. It is not anyone famous, and it is not anyone who has done anything 'great' in the most traditional sense of that word. It is an ordinary person who I think has shown great courage in the face of the most horrible circumstances. The person I would like to be is my sister Carolyn. Carolyn lost her husband, Chris Panatier on 9/11. He worked for Cantor Fitzgerald in the WTC. The reason I would want to be Carolyn is because I believe she showed great strength and courage at the time of the tragedy and continues to do so. Carolyn and Chris have two children, Annie 7 and Christopher 5. With all that she was going through at the time she made sure to comfort her children before seeking her own comfort. She kept the routine for the kids, dinner, baths, and a bedtime story. She got up everyone morning and kissed her kids and gave them breakfast and took them to school. All this was an effort to keep things as normal as possible for them while we all prayed that Chris would be found and brought home to his family. When they asked questions about Daddy, and his 'building that broke' she explained as best she could that people were looking for Daddy. When the awful time came to explain to them that Daddy would not be able to come home she assured them that the very last thing he said was how much he loved Mommy, Annie and Christopher. When she held his Memorial Service she spent more time comforting others. She made a point of speaking with everyone who attended to thank them for coming. In the months that followed she has not had an easy time, the holidays were extremely tough. But she decorated the house for the kids, she shopped so Santa could come for them and she has done everything possible to make things good and normal. Their lives were torn up enough by the death of their father, she wanted to make sure that she could keep all the other aspects of their lives running smoothly. She continues to do this. Carolyn's life was turned upside down on 9/11. Prior to this date she had a husband and the children had a father that she, Annie and Christopher planned on spending the rest of their lives with. They had a lifetime ahead of them. They had been together since high school, over 20 years. This past July 2002 would have been their 12th wedding anniversary.

We all, obviously, wish 9/11 had never happened. I don't wish this kind of pain, turmoil and anguish on anyone. But I would choose Carolyn as the person I would like to be because of the way she held herself and her family together when it would have been easier to fall apart. I would like to be Carolyn because of the strength and courage she showed in the face of the tragedy that consumed her life. She didn't cure a disease, or achieve world peace, but she got up and she went on and she keeps on doing so. She put aside her pain and grief and she makes the world as good a place as she can for her children. To me that is the greatest accomplishment of all".

Now I know that that was a very emotionally charged response, so read the remainder, I promise you, they are lighter hearted.

Judy: "I would be a healthier me. I figure everyone has his or her own baggage to carry or cross to bear. No one has a perfect life. I love my life. I thank God for it everyday. But my constant health problems do bog me down and that's why I would still want to be me, just healthier. As long as we are dreaming here, I would like to be two inches taller too".

Evie: "Why that's a toughie! Can it be a few? Diane Chambers of Cheers, to be with Sam Malone. I would love to be a nurse on ER so I could hook up with Dr. Carter. I'd like to be a female Neil Young— to have that amazing talent and be so cool at the same time. I am sure there are more, but these are the first ones that come to mind".

Sophie: "If I could be anyone, I choose me. I have not always made the best decisions in my life, but I am happy with how things have turned out. If I could talk to someone, it would be Marilyn Monroe. She had a strength and a vulnerability to her that I would love to explore".

Ellen: "My Great Aunt Dot. She was spunky, courageous and strong in her beliefs. She was sensitive, kind, caring and determined. She became a widow at the age of 31 and never remarried. She never once complained and was able to make a complete life for herself. She was one of my best friends. She truly lived what she believed in and never let anyone tell her different".

Erin: "Mother Teresa is the first person that comes to mind. I think if I could ever be that selfless and kind that I will have achieved much in my life".

DeniseB: "I don't know, but I would like to try living in the 1800's or the late 1940's, after the war".

BethL: "I have many heroes. I admire anyone who has had the courage to reach a goal".

Tracy: "I would be me". Well put Tracy!

Jenny: "I don't know that I would be anyone else. There are lots of people I would like to be like, kind of a composite of Gandhi and Bette Davis, a person who makes the world a better place while kickin' ass, takin' names and being fabulous".

Elena: "Maybe someone like Eleanor Roosevelt, a person who made their name by doing for others".

Priscilla: "Never gave it a thought because I really wouldn't want to be anyone else. I am truly happy with who I am".

BethR: "If I could be anyone else, it would certainly have to be someone alive. Why would I want to be someone dead? (She is such a smartass) I am always thinking 'Boy, wouldn't it be great to be so and so' But if I had to take someone's life soup to nuts—no thanks. Everyone has their crosses to bear—they just don't always show them to the world. If I could piece together a few parts from several different people's lives, now that's another story"!

Nancy: "I thought this was a toughie and couldn't come up with an answer".

Susan: I will not reprint the whole response.

DeniseW: "There is no one else I would rather be".

CHAPTER 7—WHAT IS THE BEST THING ABOUT TURNING 40? WHAT IS THE WORST?

This is the question that turned up all the great adjectives. Let's deal with the best part first. Here is where all those great adjectives came up. You have your "freeing", your "wiser and more mature" throw in "wisdom" and the ever popular "confidence". Kind of makes 40 sound pretty darn attractive doesn't it? It seems like we all feel that we have finally "come into our own". Most of us, like Tracy, have given up on the idea that we want to please everyone and that we want everyone to like us. We all feel that we are worthy individuals and if someone else cannot see that, well too bad for them! This may sound like a simple thing, but in fact, as girls, most of us were raised to be the peacekeeper, to play nice and make everyone feel comfortable, often at our own expense. Suck it up for the greater good. Those days are done. Many of us have made our peace with the past, whether dealing with the run of the mill issues of self-confidence, people pleasing, body image, sexuality or just plain speaking up for ourselves to the much more difficult issue of abuse. We feel that we could not, or were not equipped, to come to terms with these things in our 20's, or even our 30's. I guess this goes back to that "wisdom comes with age" adage. It seems to be rooted in truth. So by far the best thing about 40 seems to be the comfort level, or acceptance, we have attained for ourselves. Everyone interviewed actually seems to like themselves, flaws and all. We have even accepted or embraced our flaws, or just plain learned to live with them. They do, after all, give us character.

What is the worst part about turning 40? Only a few of the girls even answered this part of the question. That in itself means the positive aspects must far outweigh the negative. Several of us were able to come up with just a few negative things worth mentioning. Ellen, Sophie, Erin, BethL and Tracy all are concerned with the physical changes that age inevitably brings, such as the slowing down of our metabolism. That is a biggie. We miss the days of beer, pretzels, pizza and takeout Chinese. None of us seem to be able to dance until 4am anymore. Consequently, most of us exercise on a regular basis and fight the good fight for eating right. Erin and BethL miss that youthful glow. Moisturizing has become a very heated topic of conversation in our age group. Then there is what we feel is the label that society gives us, *old*. Clearly we don't view ourselves as old, clearly 70 is old, not 40. But Susan and Priscilla do make a good point in that many others, especially those younger than us; feel that 40 is indeed *old*.

I guess my favorite answer to this question is going to have to be Tracy's response. When asked, **"What is the best thing about turning 40? What is the Worst"?** Tracy gave what I believe to be a fairly universal answer: "The best thing about turning 40 is that I really don't care what people think of me. I am who I am, and if you like me that's great. If you don't, that's OK too. The worst thing about turning 40 would have to be that my metabolism is sooooooo much slower than in my 20's and early 30's. I hate to have to watch what I eat and exercise, but now I have to".

I just think most women feel this way. I would like to add that Tracy is one of those tall slender people who we all spend our lives hoping that someday they will face the same daily battle of the bulge that the rest of us do. She still is, even after 3 children, tall and slender.

Here's what the rest of the girls wrote:

Judy: "I find turning 40 freeing. I try not to sweat the small stuff too much. In my 20s and early 30s a bad haircut could literally ruin my day. Now my attitude is 'oh well, it'll grow'. I think the older I get the more confident and secure I am becoming. I no longer need or want everyone to like me. I make better, more informed decisions. I speak up for myself more. I am eliminating a lot of negativity from my life and that includes negative people. I have never been happier. I think all these things are achieved with age. The worst part of turning 40 for me is health issues. I am constantly dealing with some ailment, arthritis, hypothyroidism etc. and though they are treatable sometimes it just all gets to me. I feel like I need God to send me a wake up call every now and again to remind me how lucky I really am".

Evie: "The best thing is that with age comes wisdom. I feel better about myself now than I have in years, so to me 40 isn't looking too bad. The worst? Why couldn't I have felt this way when I was younger and could have appreciated what I had then"?

Sophie: "The best thing about being 40 is that I can finally see an end to my official working life. I am starting to look forward to retirement. Luckily I was in the right place at the right time and began investing at age 30 and I will be able to take it easy and do some traveling. I will be able to make it on some small part-time job. I can retire in 6 years. The worst thing about turning 40 is that I can feel my body slowing down and since I am in the military I have to constantly keep running and ensure my weight stays in check, which is actually good because otherwise I would probably let it slip".

Ellen: "That I get a party. I have never had a party for my birthday. I want a big one. Oh, and yes I do feel many of my daily life interactions throughout the years have made me wiser and more mature. The worst part about turning 40 is probably recognizing that the physical aging process is really starting to kick in". In order to be a good friend I am taking it upon myself to make sure that Ellen's husband Bob throws her a BIG party. I hope I am invited.

Erin: "Not sure about the best, but the worst is the loss of my youthful looking skin".

DeniseB: "The best part of turning 40 is that I still have so much to look forward to. The worst part would have to be that I don't have any children".

BethL: "The best thing is that now I have confidence in myself as a person both professionally and personally. I care less about what other people think and more about what makes me happy. The worst thing is having wrinkles and the grey hairs that I have been covering for years".

Tracy: "The best thing about turning 40 is that I really don't care what other people think of me. I am who I am, and if you like me that's great, and if you don't that's ok too. The worst thing is my metabolism is sooooooo slow. I hate to have to watch what I eat and exercise, but now I have to".

Jenny: "The two W's. Wisdom is the best part and wrinkles is definitely the worst".

Elena: "The best thing about turning 40 is the confidence level that has come with age. I don't care what other people think of me. I make decisions that are good for me and my family and try to forget about other people's negative reactions (I would not do something that would hurt someone else).

Priscilla: "The best thing is having older children. Ashlee and Parker are going on 13 and 12. I love talking to them and enjoy their company as young people. What is the worst? Probably the fact that society views 40 as 'mid-life' implying that it is all down hill from here"!

BethR: Age 39. Married to Joe forever. Beth is Mrs. Mom. Even my son Tommy was calling her Momma for a while. She has 3 children, Kelsey 11, and the twins, Emily and Jack age 8, born coincidentally on the same day as my Tommy, May 21, 1994. Beth is a Pediatric Nurse by training and I call her all the time for advice. She is an amazing Mom with lots of patience. She is creative and crafty (I hate people with talent). Beth knows way too much about me. I need to keep her close so she doesn't spill any of my dirty little secrets. Fortunately for me I have quite a bit on her too. Beth grew up in Rockville Centre, New York where her parents, Mary and Ron raised Beth along with Bob, Eileen, Rich, Mary and Billy. She attended Villanova University where she met Joe.

Nancy: "I can't really think of anything great about turning 40 except it beats the alternative! The worst part is that people perceive you differently when you are 40. They think you can't relate to people in there 20's and 30's anymore. I relate better to younger people than to older ones".

Susan: "Best or worst thing about turning 40? The best thing is probably that we have survived our 20s and 30s. We have experienced many different things. We have made mistakes and hopefully learned from them. The worst thing? We are no longer considered young. We may feel young, and think young, but the only other people who agree with us are people our age or older. Younger people consider us old. I hired a girl last week that was born the year I graduated high school (1981). So I tell her this and she says to me 'my mom graduated then too'! It made me feel so old".

DeniseW: "The best thing about turning 40 is being an actual 'adult'. The worst thing about it is being an actual 'adult'". Note from author: I like that.

CHAPTER 8—HOW IS YOUR HEALTH? WHAT DO YOU DO TO STAY HEALTHY? HOW HAVE YOUR EXERCISE, EATING AND SKINCARE HABITS CHANGED SINCE YOUR EARLY TWENTIES?

What we basically learn from question #8 is that we all pretty much abused our bodies in our 20's and even our early 30's, and some of us still are, see Susan's response. It also seems that we are all blessed in the fact that we are all pretty healthy. I think this is a really important issue and needs to be discussed at length. So I will. It seems whenever a group of us girls get together we are discussing our health. This topic usually comes right after bitching about our husbands and kids. All of us have bitched endlessly about our periods and how they have changed for the worse, how they are longer and heavier, more unreliable, meaning we no longer have any idea when we are going to get it. We have all noticed PMS has become a nightmare, rivaled only by the hormonal stage of puberty. I guess, we are kind of going through a reverse puberty. I was surprised no one mentioned this though since as I have stated, I have had this conversations with Ellen, Evie, Jenny, Erin, Nancy, BethR, and

Nancy. Maybe menstrual cycles will fit more into question #14 (menopause). A few of us are noticing some change in our overall health. Jenny speaks of having back and stomach problems creeping up on her in the past few years. BethL, DeniseB and I are all dealing with Hypothyroidism, a chronic disease most people just think of as a slow metabolism, but which in fact affects your entire system. Elena had a recent scare with some lumps she had removed, but thank God were not cancerous. Overall we are a healthy bunch. Evie, Sophie, BethR, Jenny and Elena and DeniseB are all taking a proactive roll in their health. They are making a concerted effort to eat better and exercise more.

The one thing that I think everyone mentioned, and I find this interesting, is the slowing down of her metabolism. Tracy and Erin both feel that they can no longer indulge in junk food as often without paying a heavy price on the scale (pun intended). Everyone mentioned that they have to work harder to lose weight, and some, like Tracy, have vowed to lose that nasty last couple of baby pounds. Just for the record, the average American woman retains 5-10 lbs. per child. Most of the women I know, and certainly the ones interviewed here, have perhaps, and I stress the word perhaps, retained 5-10 pounds after the birth of ALL their children. A few have returned, with hard work, to pre-baby weight. I guess all this is inevitable, though disappointing. I am happy to report that there is a lot of exercising going on here. Evie, as I believe I mentioned earlier, is doing Yoga and Pilate's. These particular exercises are great for women, especially in our "exclusive age group". For those of you not familiar with either, both Yoga and Pilate's concentrate of a series of stretching and breathing routines. The object is to promote flexibility, strength and a healthy mind. Our girls in uniform, BethL and Sophie probably, ok definitely, have the most rigorous exercise routine. BethL mentions her PT, or to us laymen, Physical Fitness Training, is 3-5 times a week and consists of running 10-15 miles and weight training. It sounds like the Army has tapped into the secret of staying fit—a combination of cardio and strength training. We could all take a tip here. Cardio as we know, is necessary to keep us heart healthy and it tends to burn calories and fat, but nothing will tone those hard to reach spots like your inner thighs quite the way weights will.

There are also added benefits to using weights (which can be dumbbells, body bars or strap ons) it is great for bone density. We ladies approaching 40 are losing bone density at an alarming rate due to aging and loss of estrogen. One of the best things we can do for our bones is strength and weight training. This does not necessarily mean pumping iron. Once or twice a week for 30-60 min. or even 10 minutes a day a 3-5 times a week is beneficial. You do not need to lift heavy weights, use 2-8 lbs., depending on your skill level. Begin with a few repetitions a day (check any women's magazine, especially SELF or FITNESS, but Vogue, In-Style, ELLE, Redbook will all have a few pages dedicated to this type of exercise) at a low weight and work yourself up to a level you are comfortable with. The greatest thing about weights is that you can see results, especially in the arm and back area, within weeks. So we get to look better and do something good for our bodies at the same time. Weights are good for our muscles, flexibility and our bones. They are easy to use and inexpensive. But let's not forget the easiest exercise of all, walking. It's good for you and easy. It can be done anywhere and for the cost of a pair of sneakers, you are set. My advice, find an exercise you enjoy doing and get busy. Stay healthy. It is really so important.

Here's a word that came up in just about everyone's answer— moisturizer. Ladies, moisturizer is your friend. So is sunscreen, which I am happy to report is also widely used. Wrinkles or fine lines (there that makes is sound more dignified doesn't it?) seem to be our biggest skincare issue. I guess we are all trying to stave off those horrible wrinkles that are appearing around our eyes. I think the commercial term for this is "Crows Feet". Isn't that just lovely? Have you ever seen real crow's feet? They are disgusting. I suggest we continue to use the term "fine lines". The only problem with that is now that we are approaching 40 we can no longer really hide our "fine lines" with a dab of concealer. I actually love what Susan said about makeup. She no longer wears it. None of us really do, a bit of blush, lipstick and mascara for daytime. That's really it. This tells me that even though we are making an effort to slow down any additional "fine lines" that may find their way onto our faces, we must all be pretty content with the way our faces are now. Not one respondent cited any of the latest trends in skincare as an option. No one appears to be using Botox or having any of those microderm abrasion facials, laser treatments or facelifts. Read on for more details.

These are all really good answers. All of us are taking action. Well, maybe Susan and Nancy need a little push! We are exercising and eating right and we are desperately trying to moisturize away our wrinkles. None of us bake in the sun, and sunscreen use is way up. We are Madison Ave's wet dream. We are the 40-year old demographic with money to spend. Anyway, first prize for favorite response goes to......Priscilla. She took a very sad, life-altering event and walked away with a valuable life lesson. Here is what I mean.

When asked: *"How is your health? What do you do to stay healthy? How have your exercise, eating and skincare habits changed since your early 20s and early 30s?"* Priscilla responded: "My health is excellent. Having my Dad die so young of a heart attack has increased my awareness of heart healthy lifestyle. I watch what I eat and exercise daily. I am also careful about sunscreen and moisturizer. I use them daily. I like Oil of Olay the best (and it is made by Procter and Gamble the company I work for).

Here is what the rest of us had to say on this topic.

Judy: "It is all about my health! I honestly do not know anyone who tries harder (though unsuccessfully) to stay healthy than me. I drink 64 oz. of water daily. I eat a minimum of 5 servings of fruits and veggies a day, very little red meat or dairy, lots of chicken and fish and have even cut way down, though not eliminated, on my bread/carbs intake. I exercise 4-5 times a week cardio with weights. I take calcium supplements, well most of the time anyway. Yet here I am at 39 recently diagnosed with Hypothyroidism and Arthritis. While neither are advanced cases, both are chronic and I am learning to live with the discomfort and fatigue. What I decided a few years back is I want to control whatever aspects of my health that I can because so much of it is just beyond my control. I eat better now than I did in my 20s or 30s. I have always exercised and taken good care of my skin. I have not used soap since I turned 30. I am definitely more into moisturizer these days. I am a big fan of anything with retinol in it".

Evie: "My health is better now than ever. This past year I have been doing Yoga, Pilate's and running after a toddler, enough to keep anyone young and fit. My eating habits are changing slowly. I have been eating more salads, veggies and a fruit than ever before, unfortunately chocolate still has a stronghold over my willpower. I recently joined Weight Watchers and my habits are improving. My skincare habits have changed too. I use a lot more sunscreen than I used to, and any product that claims to tighten or smooth wrinkles or brighten your skin I will try. I also drink a ton of water".

Sophie: "My overall health is good considering my family history of diabetes, high blood pressure, cholesterol and cancer. Since I am in the military, I have comprehensive health coverage. I really like to sleep in the mornings, so I have to be more creative about exercising. I don't have to exercise with a group except for once each week. On my own I try to do Cardio 2 times a week and strength training 2 times. I actually need more but my husband and I do try and walk in the evenings. I recognize that staying physical is an effort I have to make myself do. When I ignore it or slow down I feel it quickly. I feel heavy and tired. I have recently let my weight go and I am need to really focus to lose it. It is not as easy as it was in my 20's or even my 30's. My husband ensures that we eat fruit and vegetables, and I make sure we don't have red meat everyday".

Ellen: "Great health. I exercise fairly regularly. I have a strict skincare routine that I try and maintain. In my 20's and early 30's I did not take such good care of myself. I didn't give my future health much thought. I also did not know many people with health problems. As I have gotten older I have come across many people who have had this or that health issue and it has helped me focus on the importance of taking care of myself".

Erin: "My health is good. In my 20's and early 30's I didn't have exercise, eating or skincare habits—everything just sort of fell into place. Not anymore!!!!!! The past couple of years I have noticed a big change. I can't eat whatever I want anymore and if I do the scale will tell me I shouldn't have. Also, moisturizer has become very important to me".

DeniseB: "My health is fine. I am now exercising more than I used to and am watching what I eat. My skincare habits have remained unchanged".

BethL: "I am Hypothyroid. I was diagnosed at 23, which is 10-15 years earlier than the average woman. It is a manageable chronic disease that has just become a part of my life. I have physical fitness training 3-5 days a week. The Army is serious about this, especially at Fort Bragg, NC. I run approximately 10-15 miles per week and lift weights. I try to eat healthy and drink alcohol only moderately. I do more weight training now than in my 20s-30s to stave off the fat and low bone density that has plagued my mother who is also hypothyroid. I have had to use moisturizers throughout my 30s (Hypothyroids tend to have dry skin and brittle hair and nails). I use more sunscreen, drink more water and even wear big hats outdoors".

Tracy: "As I mentioned in the previous question, my health is good, but I am going to make a true effort to lose that baby weight. It's really about time since my oldest is 11 and the youngest is five. I figure I gained 3-5 pounds with each kid".

Jenny: "I am much more conscious of my health, and the proactive role I can play in it, than I was in my 20s. I never exercised or watched what I ate, never took particularly good care of myself. Then, I started to realize I could do things to positively impact my health. I also watched my parents having health problems, just the normal aces and pains that have always been associated with growing older—arthritis and things like that. And I thought no way. I do not want that to be me. Around 30, I started having problems—throwing my back out, stomach problems, and that was a wake up call for me. So I started really taking care of my health, and I learned I could control it. I will say that it is easier to do that in your early 30s. Women look great then, and they are able to achieve that with some reasonable diet and exercise. At 39, it is much harder to see results.

But I am more motivated to keep it up—I think, 'Damn it'. I will continue to fit into these pants".

Elena: "Luckily I am a healthy person. At 35 I went for my first physical with a General Practitioner (GP) in over 10 years. I had had children and seen my OBGYN, but not gone for a full physical. Lumps had to be removed from my breast and possible cancerous moles removed which really made me stop to think how healthy (and lucky) I was. I had been trying to get pregnant again and was using that as an excuse to be overweight. When I realized that it may never happen, and that I was very uncomfortable with my self-image, I started watching what I ate and began a regular exercise routine. I began feeling better about my health and myself but did not ever get to a point that I felt "great". I kept this up for two years until my look took a complete turn around about 8 months ago. Joe and I found out I was pregnant with TWINS! I have been unable to continue my exercise program because this has been a much more difficult pregnancy than my other 3. I have tried to maintain good eating habits. My goal is to look better after this pregnancy even though I will be almost 40, than I did after my others in my early 30s. As far as skincare is concerned, shortly after turning 30 I realized I should be taking better care of my skin. Fine lines were appearing and sun damage from those teen years of aluminum foil on album covers and baby oil was taking its toll. I stopped using whatever soap was on sale and began using skin creams etc…At around 35 I read a magazine article that said all the products I had been using were really meant for younger skin than mine (ouch) so I started a new, more appropriate routine. I am not hung up on it. I use the right soap and moisturizer and sunscreen".

Priscilla: "My health is excellent. Having my Dad die so young of a heart attack has increased my awareness of heart healthy lifestyle. I watch what I eat and exercise daily. I am also careful about sunscreen and moisturizer. I use them daily. I like Oil of Olay the best (and it is made by Procter and Gamble the company I work for)".

BethR: "Thankfully my health is excellent. I have no health problems that I know of and no complaints. I have exercised very consistently since I was 20 something, not that it shows! Exercise is my stress reducer and I really feel it if I don't get to the gym. My eating habits have definitely changed. I am much more conscious of what I eat and what my family eats. I really try to eat a healthy balanced diet, but I have no willpower. As far as skincare is concerned I am definitely lagging. Most nights I don't even wash my face. It is all I can do to get my teeth brushed! I wash my face in the shower with whatever is there, I usually use Dove which is ok. I am trying to remember to moisturize. I notice I do better in the summer since I know it has sunscreen in it".

Nancy: "My health is great (so far) despite all the crap I eat. To stay healthy I look at healthy, slim people in magazines and wish I were like them. That's it".

Susan: "How is my health, etc...? So far my health is pretty good. I don't get the flu. I get one cold a year. I have never taken a sick day from work. What do I do to achieve this great feat? Nothing. I must say I don't live the healthiest lifestyle. I work in a bar/restaurant. I work crazy hours and get very little sleep. I eat most of my meals on the run or standing up. I don't even eat at the normal meal times because that is when I am the busiest at work. I still have poor eating habits. I eat lots of fried foods and junk food. I have gotten better than I was in college though. I no longer consider chips and dip as a food group, although chocolate is still pretty high up in my food pyramid. I drink excessive amounts of diet soda and iced tea. I smoke cigarettes. I very rarely eat fruits and vegetables and don't exercise at all. I have no idea how I have managed to stay this healthy".

DeniseW: "My health is great. I don't do too much to stay healthy. I eat the same foods I always have, though not as much fried food or red meat. My skincare habits have changed in that now I use a lot more moisturizer and sunscreen".

CHAPTER 9—HAVE YOU EVER LIED ABOUT YOUR OCCUPATION? WHY OR WHY NOT?

This may sound like a silly question, but I think we all know people who have the need to make themselves sound "better" or "indispensable". They lie about their title, their paycheck, and their bonus and, of course, their age. It is worth mentioning that some people just seem to lie about everything. Most of the time we actually know they are lying and this makes them more frustrating to listen to. Then there is the "little white lie". Anyone who claims to have never told one of these is a "big fat liar". We all embellish. It is human nature. On an interview we are likely to "stretch the truth". We may add a few extra responsibilities on to our resume so it sounds more "professional". As long as you don't go overboard, for instance claiming to be CFO (Chief Financial Officer) when you are the Book Keeper, it's acceptable. I know several people in Human Resources and they say that it is almost expected. Just don't make yourself sound too good to be true, because the old saying does hold true here. "If someone sounds too good to be true, they probably are". Once again, I am happy to say that this group of ladies appears to be painfully honest. We all feel that the work we do or have done is worthwhile. Susan is happy in the Restaurant business, and may I say we do all owe her our gratitude. We need restaurants we all need a break now and then. Jenny loves teaching. BethL and Sophie are enjoying rewarding military careers. We owe a big debt of gratitude here. Tracy, Ellen and Evie are all stay-at-home Moms who chose to give up careers on Wall St, in Insurance and in Advertising respectively to do so. All mentioned feeling that you should take pride in whatever you do, as long as it is honest works. Every job has a reason. We need our Garbage men, our Newspaper carriers, our Lawyers, our Teacher and our Moms. They all perform a valuable service.

Out of the 15 ladies interviewed only Elena and DeniseW admit to ever lying about their occupations. For DeniseW it is a bit of a self-esteem issue in her younger days, the feeling that she wasn't measuring up. For Elena it is kind of funny, which is probably why hers is my choice for favorite response. When asked ***"Have you ever lied about your occupation? Why or Why not"?*** Elena responded: "In a way I have! I am a teacher. However, I am not a working teacher! I worked so hard to be a teacher and a good one at that. I made the decision to give up my career to be home with my children. I do not regret it for one second. BUT when people ask what I do, I invariably say 'I am a teacher'. The years I spent teaching became such an enormous part of my life. I loved it so much. It feels like lying now because it has been so many years since I have actually 'taught'". Now, we can look at this one of two ways. Either Elena is the only one in the group who has lied about her occupation (it is really such a little white lie it is almost not worth mentioning) OR and I am stressing the OR here, Elena is the only one of the bunch HONEST enough to admit that she has, let's just say, stretched the truth a bit. To be forthright here, Elena has chosen two of the most demanding professions known to man. Actually both are predominantly FEMALE professions. Motherhood is limited to females of course. Elena is the mother of 4 (soon to be six) and is or was, depending on your definition of the word "lie", a teacher. I don't understand why teachers are not the most respected, revered and highest paid professionals we have. When you think of the priceless commodity, namely our children's education, that we are entrusting them with, they should be better compensated. Personally I prefer to have the best, brightest and most dedicated teaching my children— wouldn't you? And if you were lucky enough to have had Elena or Jenny for a teacher, let me tell you, that is exactly what you got. But I digress, that is another issue entirely. So let's get back to why Elena would lie? Isn't being the mother of 4 children job enough? For most women that would be job "too much". Myself included. I think in Elena's case it is not so much to bolster her ego, as it is that she IS a teacher. I mean that in the figurative sense of the word. It is a personality trait with her, just as kindness or generosity would be. Some people are just destined for this profession. Elena is one of them. So even though she admits to "lying" well, let's cut her some slack. I hope Elena is not mad at me for choosing her as my favorite response for this question. See, part of me still doesn't want to upset people. At least not the ones I love.

OK, here are the remaining responses. You decide if these ladies are lying or not????

Judy: "I don't think I had ever lied about my occupation. I lied about many things while drinking beers at Jeremy's at South St. Seaport. I claimed that red-headed, alabaster skinned Julie was my twin sister and that we were each raised by one of our divorced parents and that I was putting Julie through Law School. But not about my occupation I never saw a reason too. I have worked on Wall St and on Madison Ave and was always proud of what I was doing".

Evie: "No, I don't believe so. I have always worked in various aspects of advertising and thought that it was pretty interesting stuff".

Sophie: "I have never lied about my occupation. I have been very focused on pursuing my Psychology degree and have bemoaned the fact that so much education is required in order to practice. I have always enjoyed the reaction I get from people when I tell them I am in the Army. I am short (62") and have long hair, and people tend to think of the military as an unusual occupation".

Ellen: "No. I have not lied about my occupation. I think throughout my 20s I was fairly successful, at least by my own standards, and I enjoyed working".

Erin: "The best answer to this question had to come from my son Tommy who read the question over my shoulder and replied 'You don't really have an occupation, do you'? I stay at home with my 3 sons. I do it well most of the time and they are happy so I never had any reason to lie". Note from the author here! Erin—read that kid the riot act! He needs to know that Mommy is a full-time, plus weekends and holidays, career choice!

DeniseB: "No I have never been ashamed of any job I have had".

BethL: "No. I have always been proud to earn an honest living. I was employed as a maid and worked at a fast food restaurant in high school. I waited tables and served my fellow students all through college (who can forget the nasty dish room at Serra Hall)? Being an officer in the United States Army is one of the proudest accomplishments of my life. It feels good to be one of the 'good gals'".

Tracy: "No. Being a stay-at-home Mom is very important. Some days I do it better than others. At times I wish I were out of the house more, but this is the job I chose for myself".

Jenny: "No, I've never wanted to lie about my occupation. I may have lied about my name (to guys in my college days), but not my job. Seriously, it never even occurred to me. Is that something you do because you're embarrassed or bored with your career choice? I guess when I was younger, before I had what I would really term a 'career', I didn't care what people thought. Since then, I've always been proud of what I do for a living. I think everyone should be as long as it's honest. If you're a Garbage Man, you're a garbage man, you keep things clean, and we need you. What's wrong with that"?

Elena: "In a way I have! I am a teacher. However, I am not a working teacher! I worked so hard to be a teacher, and a good one at that. I made the decision to give up my career to be home with my children. I do not regret it for one second. BUT when people ask what I do, I invariably say 'I am a teacher'. The years I spent teaching became such an enormous part of my life. I loved it so much. It feels like lying now because it has been so many years since I have actually 'taught'".

Priscilla: "No, I am proud of what I do and am proud of the company I work for. Procter and Gamble is an awesome company and I really wouldn't want to work for anyone else at this point in my career".

BethR: "I have never lied about my occupation, although it has been a long time since I really had one outside my home. People don't seem to really ask me what I do. I guess most of the people I come in contact with at this point in my life are either other stay-at-home Moms, or work only part-time. I don't seem to cross paths with too many full-time working Moms".

Nancy: "I've never lied about what I do. Even though I always feel like I am juggling 20 balls in the air and they are ready to crash down on me at any moment, I truly love working outside the home. It suits my multi-tasking, manic-personality".

Susan: "Lied about my job? Can't say I ever have. I don't see the need to lie about my job. I worked for computer company for 8 years and then started working in the restaurant business. I do what I do. It is nothing to be ashamed of or embarrassed about. If no one did my job there would be no restaurants for people to go and eat".

DeniseW: "I think when I was younger I did. I always felt I was not quite up to par as my peers".

CHAPTER 10—HAVE YOU EVER LIED ABOUT YOUR AGE? WHY OR WHY NOT?

The Ladies seem to be split down the middle on this one. Susan, Jenny, Tracy, BethL and I all admit to lying about our ages, but not in the way that you would think. We are all going way back here, to the days of yore so to speak. When eighteen was the legal drinking age, and none of us were eighteen. We all had fake ID and used it proudly. So in these cases we lied about being OLDER! This really isn't what I was after, although I answered this way myself. What I really wanted to know is if any of us had lied about being YOUNGER, and if so, why? I never understood why anyone would try and say they were younger. My thoughts here are that people may look at you and think "35? This woman does not look good for 35. She looks at least 40". While most of us could probably get away with claiming to be a year or two younger, 5 years, or more can be pushing it. Nancy admits to shaving 7 years off her age when she is out with her best friend, an actress. As for the rest of the group Erin, Tracy and Ellen feel that they have earned every year and are proud of it. I think this is a great attitude. BethR says if she ever had a really good reason maybe then she would lie about her age. What I like is that so many of the responses caused the ladies to wonder, "Why would I lie"? Forty is certainly nothing to be ashamed of. The alternative is not particularly good. Maybe society in general is forming a new, more positive, more fabulous look at 40. Maybe today's 40 year old women is helping make this possible. I guess this question kind of mirrors the previous one, proving again that they are a pretty honest bunch.

The responses were all very similar here so choosing a favorite was difficult. I am going to go with Sophie. When asked, **"Have you ever lied about your age? Why or why not"?** Sophie writes: "I don't remember ever lying about my age. I look young for my age and generally like telling people how old I am because they usually don't believe me. I also don't act my age. I embarrass my teens and think this is fun. I have only been married for 10 years and still love being affectionate with husband and that drives my kids crazy, especially my 17-year-old daughter. This makes it even more fun".

Sophie holds onto those things that keep her young, including being silly. I think being silly is a good thing.

Since we are all so painfully honest, here is what we 'fessed up to:

Judy: "I never lie about my age now. I think it's silly. I have always wanted to be older. I am a December birthday and most of my friends were older than me. When I was a teenager I had fake ID so I could get into bars, so I lied then. Most people think I am a few years younger than I am now. I was proofed, carded whatever you call it, until I was 28. My mom doesn't look her age, so I guess I have her to thank".

Evie: "No, but I've often joked about wanting to be younger, but I guess everyone does that now and then".

Sophie: "I don't remember ever lying about my age. I look young for my age and generally like telling people how old I am because they usually don't believe me. I also don't act my age. I embarrass my teens and think this is fun. I have only been married for 10 years and still love being affectionate with husband and that drives my kids crazy, especially my 17-year-old daughter. This makes it even more fun".

Ellen: "Nope. No reason to. I am who I am, and with age comes respect".

Erin: "I have never lied about my age because I have earned every year".

DeniseB: "No, I never saw any reason to lie about my age. I think I may have lied as a teenager when I first started going to bars, but I don't think that is what you are really asking".

BethL: "When I was younger I used to lie about being older. I didn't want people not to take me seriously because of my age. I thought if they felt I was too young that they would not respect my opinion (that, and I wanted to get into bars). I think that I look good for my age and don't mind telling people how old I am. Age is just a number"

Tracy: "I have only lied about my age to buy beer before I turned 18. Since then, I would have to say, no. I am not embarrassed or ashamed of my age".

Jenny: "Sure, in high school I used my sister's ID to get into bars, but since then I haven't. Like I say, usually I'm the other way around. I am the person telling everyone how old I am. I'll let you in on a little secret. I know the older generation always thinks the generation after them is inferior, but I think it's more than that—we're cooler, much cooler than kids today. I don't think it is possible to be truly cool unless you have experienced the 60s, at least to some extent. So I don't want anyone believing I am a Gen-Xer. That would mean I am tragically un-hip".

Elena: "Not in the way that you would think. My two close friends had their birthdays in January. My birthday doesn't happen until

November. Since we always celebrate our birthdays together I tend to refer to myself as being a year older than I actually am! (I plan on stopping this when I turn 40 though). I have never lied to make myself seem younger because I feel pretty confident that I don't look 40".

Priscilla: "No, but I am thrilled when I get compliments about my age. For example, 'You don't look old enough to have a kid in Junior High' that is my favorite one".

BethR: "I don't recall ever lying about my age. I just have never felt the need. I am constantly surprised by anyone who would bother to lie about occupation or age. Why do they? Maybe if I thought of a good reason to I would"???

Nancy: "I only lie about my age when I am with my best friend Mia because we're the same age but she tells everyone that she is 32".

Susan: "Lied about my age? When I was younger I lied and said I was older, primarily to get into bars. When you are a teen you want to be in your 20s. I did lie once to get on TV. When I was 22 the drinking age was being changed to 21 and a local TV station was looking for people who would be affected by the change to interview and be on the news. Elena and I both claimed to be 20 in order to get on TV.

I don't ever recall lying about my age recently. The majority of people are shocked to find out that I am almost 40. Most people put me in my early 30s. They think I am lying when I tell them my real age. Sometimes I have to pull out my license to prove it! I even got proofed buying cigarettes a few months ago. It is definitely not a bad thing that people think I look younger, and I do get a little chuckle when someone asks for my ID".

DeniseW: "No, never have. I am actually proud of my age, no one ever believes me when I tell them how old I am".

CHAPTER 11—WHO HAS HAD THE BIGGEST INFLUENCE ON YOUR LIFE?

Well, our Moms should be happy with the responses to this question. After a lifetime of arguing about everything from the clothes we wore to the men we chose to date, it seems that our mothers (followed closely by our fathers) do in fact have the greatest influence on our lives. For better or worse, our parents basically help shape our lives from infancy until, at the very least, young adulthood. So I don't really find this a surprising response. Since all the people interviewed here are women, and many of us mothers ourselves, it is also not surprising that we chose our Moms. Tracy, Elena and I chose our Moms specifically. Ellen, DeniseB and Jenny went with both parents. Since Mom is one half of 'parents' she gets credit in both categories, making Mom the run-away favorite. This makes me feel two ways. Scared to death—if I am going to have the greatest influence on my sons' lives I may need to work on my act a bit. I am going to need a whole lot more inspirational sayings and maybe even get a few eccentricities so they can poke fun at me later in life. Like I said, I need to get busy. Maybe it is different with boys, I don't know. I am still learning when it comes to this wonderful, yet mysterious gender.

Perhaps they would choose their father, and some of the pressure will be off me. I should probably mention this to my husband Michael in case he wants to get busy polishing up his act! This also makes me feel wonderful. I like the idea of shaping their little minds. That they are listening to what we say even if it appears otherwise. I guess we have all learned things positive and negative from our parents but when it comes right down to it, it is up to us to choose what we walk away with.

BethL remembers her Dad telling her that she could do or be anything she wanted. And then backed that statement up by supporting her unorthodox choices to be a Firefighter and have a career in the Army. Several of the girls mention the constant encouragement and support offered by both Moms and Dads.

The remainder of the victims, BethR, Evie, Sophie and Nancy all had interesting responses. Beth and Evie feel that their children have had the greatest influence on their lives. In these cases it seems that since our children have changed our adult lives so dramatically that how could they not be a huge influence on us? Evie feels that having Cecelia has made her stronger. BethR says her children factor into every decision she makes. Sophie and Nancy had two different influences on their lives. Sophie credits God as her greatest influence. She feels that she never would have made it through those difficult years of abuse and a troubled first marriage without prayer and God's guidance. Another answer that seems just so logical. Nancy's biggest influence was her best friend who talked her into moving to New York after college. At first glance this may not sound like the biggest influence on a persons life, but, Nancy met her husband, Matt, in New York, married him, moved to New Jersey, changed jobs and now has 2 boys with him—sometimes you have to follow a single action through to see its true repercussions.

OK we are onto favorite response here. As I mentioned, all these responses seem to me to be just so perfect. I mean how can you argue with the fact that our parents, our children, God and our best friends have had a huge influence on our lives? Is it tacky to pick my own answer? I guess with 40 questions I would have to sooner or later.

So I am going to go with me on this one. When asked the question: ***"Who has had the biggest influence on your life?"*** I responded:

Judy: "My mom has probably had the biggest influence on my life. As a young, widowed, working Mom she showed me how to be strong. My mother makes things happen. I remember her telling me once that the first New Year's Eve after my Dad died she spent alone and that made her sad. Instead of taking a chance that this would happen again she decided to host a New Years Eve party at our house every year. My mother is pro-active. She does not sit and complain or bemoan her lot in life. She is a doer. I try to be like that too. I hate people who sit and complain about every little thing without ever having made any effort to change it. My boys have also influenced my life tremendously. Talk about setting your priorities straight. As long as my children are healthy and happy, everything else seems less important".

Here are the rest of the responses:

Evie: "Another tough question. It is very hard to pick just one person. But now that I really think about it, it would have to be my daughter, Cecelia. I think a good part of the reason I am the stronger person I am now is because I needed and wanted to be strong for her. I needed to make myself better in order to be there for her. There were days, at a very low point in my life, where she was the only reason I got out of bed. She is my joy".

Sophie: "God has had the greatest influence on my life. Because of the abuse I suffered as a child, I often found comfort in the church. During all times of trouble as I went through phases in my life, church, prayer and God have been a blessing. I was raised a Roman Catholic, but did not experience abuse there. My sister was not as lucky. A parish priest ritually abused her and the effect on her life was that her belief and understanding of God were greatly diminished. I did not learn of her abuse until I was an adult. In a way I am thankful for that because I have leaned heavily on God to get through several tough times in my life. I no longer belong to the Roman Catholic Church, however, I made a very difficult decision and now am an active United Methodist member".

Ellen: "My mother and father. I often think that I would never be where I am today, and have experienced all that I have if it were not for their encouragement and support. They never let me sit around. Therefore, I do not know how to do that now. I am constantly on the go, I don't know if that is necessarily a good thing sometimes".

Erin: "My mom, whether I like it or not. I see how much influence I have on my children, how they think like me and act like me too".

DeniseB: "My parents later on in life. I never really appreciated how they treated people until I was an adult myself. Being single I think you are probably more affected by family and friends than if you are married with children. I remember when my father was sick in the hospital that he was concerned with making sure the janitor got a tip for taking out his garbage. Every person I met said what a nice man my dad was and how much fun my mother was. I think they taught me that you never really know a person until you have walked in their shoes and that you should be nice to anyone and everyone you meet".

BethL: "My father has taught me that I can do anything I set my mind to. A lot of hard work and prayer will get a person very far. I also respect my mother, but she was raised during an age when women didn't do or go to the places that I have been in my life. When I wanted to be a Firefighter, my Dad said 'good for you'; my Mom said 'why would you want to do that'? They have both taught me to be honest and hard working and are my heroes".

Tracy: "My mother"

Jenny: "I guess my parents, because everything and everyone else springs from that in a way. And I am one of those people who just wonder about what my parents would think all the time. When I hear about someone doing a nude scene in a movie or magazine, or committing a crime, I always think 'aren't they embarrassed to think their parents are going to see this'? No matter how old I get, that concern is still there". (note from author: I think the same thing, isn't that scary)?

Elena: "It would have to be my mother. I see so much of her in myself now. I hope I am emulating the parts of her that I think are the best".

Priscilla: "My mother".

BethR: "I don't think this is what you are looking for but…my kids have really been the biggest influence on my life. Boy did everything change once they came along—especially after the twins, Jack and Emily! Everything about my life changed and they continue to influence it everyday and in every choice I make. And in case you are wondering—it has definitely been for the better. I can't imagine my life without them".

Nancy: "My girlfriend Lizbeth has probably had the biggest influence on my life. She and I were college roommates in Ohio and she is the one who convinced me to move to New York City to pursue my dreams. This was so outside my comfort zone, but I am so glad I did it because otherwise I would have stayed in the Midwest and not have seen the big bold world out there".

Susan: "I think may people have influences on our lives. I don't think there was one particular person for me. If I had to pick someone it would be my parents. They built a foundation for the person I have become. They taught me to be loving and caring and gave me my values. They encouraged me when I needed it and helped prepare me to go out into the world and take care of myself. I grew up in a nice, loving home and I think that is a huge influence on a person. I think the people you become friends with are also a big influence on you. I was very lucky to find such a great group of friends. They have been there for me whenever I needed them".

DeniseW: "My husband, Alan".

CHAPTER 12—WHAT ARE THE CHARACTERISTICS THAT ATTRACTED YOU TO YOUR SPOUSE OR SIGNIFICANT OTHER? ARE THEY THE SAME OR DIFFERENT FROM THE CHARACTERISTICS THAT YOU VALUE IN THEM NOW?

It seems that we were all attracted to our husbands for as many different reasons as there are husbands! Not many of us mentioned our husbands' good looks, though Elena, BethL, DeniseW and Evie did. I am kind of surprised since that is usually the very first thing that attracts us to another person. We may learn later that they are a jerk, a bigot, a male chauvinist or a braggart, but looks are generally the impetus for that very first conversation, that casual glance or that invitation to dance. I also know just about every single husband whose wife was subjected to my questions and let me tell you, these ladies chose well. They are a good-looking group of men. I really wouldn't expect anything else from such a group of fabulous, confident, mature, exercising, moisturizing, and sexy women! God I can be so shallow. Anyway back on track here. A big turn on for our group of girls is what I call the 'Alan Alda syndrome'. What this is is that the better sense of humor a guy has, or the nicer he is, the more we are attracted to him, and the sexier he becomes. Please forgive me Alan Alda. As I just said, I have a tendency to be a bit shallow. Humor may be the ultimate aphrodisiac to this group (sorry I had to differ with Kissinger here, but 'power' didn't even get one vote!). Of the victims, Priscilla, Evie, Ellen, Tracy, Nancy, Sophie and I all mentioned our husbands' sense of humor or outgoing personality. Priscilla admits that while this may have been what attracted her to Lee in the first place, things have shifted a bit over the years. She still enjoys his outgoing, fun side, but also values his work ethic.

Those of us with children may have noticed the biggest change in our husband's character. We love our husbands for the men they were and for the men they have become. We mothers are not the only ones who have been affected by the birth of our children. For many husbands becoming a father is the ultimate wake up call. Responsibility sets in, and if we our lucky our man becomes a dependable positive role model for our children. For some men, this may include becoming the sole breadwinner. Several of us are stay-at-home Moms. We all love it and I think each one of us realizes how lucky we are to have this option. However, I do think that the burden of a family's' financial security can be a lot to place on just one person, husband or wife, mother or father. Perhaps men are a little better at assuming this role since for centuries it has been their primary role, but even as we women are taking over the work force like a tornado men's roles are changing too. Men are infinitely more involved in the lives of their children than in past generations. So many of our fathers generation and their fathers never changed a diaper, stayed alone with the kids, ran them to practices, dried their tears, helped with the homework. So while some of us may miss the carefree attitude of our youth, what we are getting in return is invaluable. Wait a minute! We don't have to be responsible, dependable adults all the time. Something as simple as taking your spouse on a date to see an Austin Power movie (any one will do they are all 'jolly good fun') can momentarily bring back those days. Give it a try; what have we got to lose?

Favorite response for question 12 goes to Elena, it's just nice, what she had to say I mean. When asked: ***"What are the characteristics that attracted you to your spouse or significant other? Are they the same or different from the characteristics that you value in them now"?*** Elena had this to say about her husband Joe: "The characteristics that attracted me most to my husband, Joe, was his sense of stability. There are so many other things, but this stands out. I remember meeting him in my 20's and knowing I would marry him and that there could be no other person for him or for me. That feeling is the same today. I am so secure with the love and trust we share and this is what makes a long-term relationship work. Of course when we met there were physical aspects too. Those do not seem so important now, though I am absolutely still attracted to him. As our relationship has changed and family and career have grown there is always something new that I value in him".

We all had a lot to say about our husbands too, and it was all good!

Judy: "I like to tell my husband that I married him for his height and blue eyes because I wanted tall, dark haired, blue eyed children. That is only partially true! I was immediately attracted to Michael's sense of humor and his eternal optimism. Michael is able to maintain his humor and positive attitude even in a difficult situation. Fertility problems are no walk in the park and throughout our whole ordeal Michael remained the upbeat and positive one. I would be in tears, sure we would never have a baby and he was still able to make me laugh. He just knew things would work out. I did not. I would have to say yes that I definitely still value these qualities in my husband. Even when we fight we make each other laugh. It is difficult to stay mad at each other when you are laughing. Our values have always been so in sync, how we raise the boys, what we want in life, and our commitment to our marriage. We really enjoy each other's company. I think we get along very well".

Evie: "Tough one Jude. I would have to say my husband's sense of humor, love of music and looks. We started as friends and just clicked. We are now separated and are in the process of re-working our relationship. He is a good father to Cecilia".

Sophie: "When I divorced my first husband after 3 years of marriage, I swore that I would never marry again. About 5 years later when I was planning to move in just a few short months I struck up a conversation with the man who is now my husband, at a gas station. I thought he looked nice and I was interested in just hanging out with him and having some fun. He quit his job and moved with the kids and me to a new state. We married 1 year after we started dating. I am drawn to him now more than ever before. We compliment one another and laugh easily, even when we argue".

Ellen: "I would have to go with his sense of self, just knowing what he wanted. Bob is a very confident individual. I love his kindness, sensitivity, sense of humor and his ability to compromise and his sense of adventure. Most of these qualities are the same, except for maybe the sense of adventure. When we disagree now I am not sure I appreciate his sense of confidence as much as I once did, it seemed like back then there was less to disagree on".

Erin: "Frank always was a good person and still is. He has good values and tries to live up to them. He is kind, honest, sincere and good with the kids. What you see is what you get with Frank. He is not materialistic at all and sometimes, I must admit, I wish he was, but this is my fault, not his".

DeniseB: "Not relevant right now".

BethL: "The expression 'you marry your father' is the first thing that comes to mind. He's as honest as a five-year-old, romantic, thoughtful and very hard-working. He is also very intelligent and truly cares about our community and country. I also think he is handsome, sexy and knows how to make me happy—in all the rooms of the house (ooh la la). Now I also see where he comes from. He is more successful (career and financially) than his parents or siblings. In my family we are all pretty even with regard to career etc...My husband is the 'parent' in his family. He is an excellent mediator and we're very good about airing grievances without starting an all-out brawl". (Note from author; someone needs to tell Beth that 5 year olds are not very honest people).

Tracy: "Fred is kind and caring and makes me laugh. He loves me for who I am. I definitely still value these qualities today".

Jenny: "Unfortunately not applicable".

Elena: "The characteristic that attracted me most to my husband, Joe, was his sense of stability. There are so many other things, but this stands out. I remember meeting him in my 20's and knowing I would marry him and that there could be no other person for him or for me. That feeling is the same today. I am so secure with the love trust we share and this is what makes a long-term relationship work. Of course when we met there were physical aspects too. Those do not seem so important now, though I am absolutely still attracted to him. As our relationship has changed and family and career have grown there is always something new that I value in him".

Priscilla: "I was initially attracted to Lee's outgoing, fun personality. As we grew older and became parents the two of us just didn't have quite as much fun. Now I admire his work ethic and his ability to persevere. We still have some fun, but not in the way we used to. Are these the same characteristics that I initially valued? I do value his work ethic now more than I did at 25. I guess I didn't realize then how important it was".

BethR: "I think the characteristics that most attracted me to Joe are probably the very things that are driving me the craziest now! There are definitely different things I look for in him now than I did 20 years ago when we first started dating. I often think about some of the decisions we made as young adults that had such far reaching effects on our lives, the college we chose, our majors, our spouse".

Nancy: "I really like the All-American, confident, preppy type (which is funny because I am the total opposite, Amerasian, somewhat funky). I fell for my husband, Matt, because he was all that and he was very funny, outgoing, intelligent and has a really good heart. With our crazy lives today it's often difficult to remember why we fell head over heals for our spouses. Now I would have to say the one thing I truly adore about him is his complete devotion and love for our boys. That means everything to me and allows me to overlook all the other stuff that is driving me nuts"!

Susan: "As I stated previously, I don't have a significant other right now. So I don't think I can answer this one".

DeniseW: "His intelligence, determination, good looks. They are actually the same qualities that I am attracted to now".

CHAPTER 13—IF YOU COULD BE A GUEST ON ANY TV SHOW, WHICH ONE WOULD IT, BE? WHY?

I don't know about you, but I could sure use something a little more lighthearted right about now! I think we were starting to get too intense. This is one of those strictly for fun questions. Boy did we get quite a few different answers! The range of TV shows chosen ran the gamut from Doctor/Hospital shows like ER, talk shows and sitcoms. There did seem to be a common thread in several answers. BethR, Erin, DeniseB and Elena all chose talk shows. Not all the same talk shows, but that particular format. I think that shows a certain self—confidence. I would even say a sense of adventure. I find that interesting because I myself would be a little afraid to be interviewed on a talk show. I would be nervous that I would make a fool out of myself. The talk show hosts mentioned, Rosie, Oprah, Johnny and Dave, have all at one time thrown the occasional curve and ask the one question that a guest just doesn't seem to want to answer. Who will ever forget the moment Jay Leno asked Hugh Grant "What the hell were you thinking"? I guess I shouldn't really be surprised that any of the girls chose a talk show, after all they were all willing to subject themselves to answer 40 rather personal questions for possible (albeit hopeful) publication. I don't think anyone could call this a shy or not talkative bunch. The rest of us seem to prefer make believe. Evie, our true ER devotee chose, true to form, ER. Sex and the City gets a couple of nods here from us ladies who miss NY and long to teeter on a pair of $450 Manolo Blaniks. For the intellectual in us West Wing gets three votes, and does anyone remember SOAP? This is truly the funniest show ever made. It starred Katherine Helmond as Jessica Tate, the matriarch of a rich, severely dysfunctional (I mean it, her daughter gives birth to the devils child and her brother-in-law the extremely talented Richard Mulligan, is abducted by aliens) yet somehow loving and hysterical family. Jenny and I used to rush back from dinner in college in order to watch it. By the end of the season we had a whole group of people joining us and quoting the characters. I believe it is now in reruns on TVLAND or some other cable channel.

It cracked me up that BethL mentioned "Love Boat" and "Fantasy Island". Everyone who participated in this book grew up on these two shows. They were as an important part of our diet as Pizza and chocolate. Talk about the ultimate in make-believe. Was anyone other than me shocked to discover that the "Love Boat" cruise took place in one weekend? These people were falling in love and getting married in 3 days and 2 nights! And Fantasy Island, now this is truly a great concept. Pay lots of money, go to a tropical island and have the mysterious and elegant Mr. Rourke fulfill your fantasy. Sheer genius. Hey, Mr. Rourke, can you publish my book?

So it seems like we all had a little fun here, indulged our wild side a bit. But my favorite answer is perhaps the simplest one, DeniseB's. When asked, *"If you could be a guest on any TV show which one would you choose? Why?"* DeniseB responded, "I would choose Johnny Carson or Dave Letterman. I really enjoy their shows and they seem to make their guests feel comfortable". As I said earlier, I just think that is an incredibly brave choice.

Check out the rest of our little fantasies:

Judy: "I really only watch a few shows. I would love to be on 'Sex and the City' as long as I get to look great and use the "F" word at least a dozen times. I would also love to be on 'West Wing'. It is my favorite show and not just because Rob Lowe is my 'crush de jour', I love that it makes me think. In the next election I am voting for Jed Bartlett for President. He is the greatest. My favorite show of all time, the greatest show ever made is 'SOAP' but it went off the air years ago".

Evie: "Easy. 'ER', so that I can work closely with Dr. Carter, and he'd fall madly in love with me and we would live happily ever after in his grandmother's mansion…" (Note from author: tell Evie to submit this as a script idea!)

Sophie: "I think it would be awesome to be on one of those forensic/crime type shows. I really get grossed out by blood, but at the same time am in awe of how science can piece together separate facts and determine fact and fiction to get down to the truth".

Ellen: "I've really had to give this one some thought. I think I would like to be on The West Wing. I find the men rather handsome and intellectually stimulating and have always been fond of the political scene. I am the type of person who likes to be 'in the know' and the people who work in the White House clearly are. I also enjoy the fast paced environment and like to fantasize about attending big galas and being able to wear beautiful dresses and having someone do my makeup".

Erin: "I would like to be on Oprah, just because I like her. I think she has good values".

DeniseB: "I would choose Johnny Carson or Dave Letterman. I really enjoy their shows and they seem to make their guests feel comfortable".

BethL: "I used to think I would like to be on the 'Love Boat' or Fantasy Island to find the man of my dreams, but now I would have to go with Third Watch or ER. Since I have already found the man of my dreams (he really is wonderful, just ask Evie) I can concentrate on others. I have always been service oriented and a bit of an adrenaline junky, so the combination of these two shows really fits the bill for me".

Tracy: "If I could be a guest on any TV show it would be 'Touched by an Angel' because I think it would be a very peaceful and spiritual experience. From what I read a majority of those who appear on this show have deep faith and I think I would benefit from being around them. Another show I would like to be a guest on is 'The West Wing'. I like the way they all appear to get along and find the workings of Washington and the White House very interesting".

Jenny: "I don't know. I guess 'Ed' or 'Scrubs' because they are fun shows. Or maybe that show Isaac Mizrahi has on cable. He seems like he'd be fun to hang around with. Really, I would like to have been on 'SOAP' (but Judy already knew that) or 'Northern Exposure' because they are the best TV shows ever made, and NE had the added attraction of John Corbett. I don't really aspire to be on a TV show, I do however, harbor a secret dream of being a caller on 'Car Talk'. I just love Click and Clack".

Elena: "Rosie O'Donnell. I don't watch too much TV. I would choose Rosie because she grew up in the same area of LI that I did and we are the same age. I feel like I can relate to her. I would also choose her because she is not your average TV personality, tall, thin, blonde and beautiful. She is so much more real".

Priscilla: "Probably one of the cooking shows like Food Nation with Bobby Flay. Food has a way of bringing people together in that 'feel-good' sort of way. It allows friends and family to get together for a meal and sometimes this simple act brings enormous satisfaction to me".

BethR: "If I could be a guest on any TV show, it would be 'The Rosie O'Donnell Show'. Because A. I like her and think she is funny. B. She seems to keep her guests at ease and I am not comfortable speaking in public C. Her interviews are usually short. She frequently gives her guests' cool prizes or great vacations! How shallow am I"?

Nancy: "I would love to be on "Sex and the City" because it is the life that all of us suburban Moms want to live, glamorous clothes, gorgeous men falling all over you, fabulous clubs and restaurants and girlfriends you can spend all your time gabbing with (without your kids jumping on your head and pulling you in 20 different directions)".

Susan "If I could be on any TV show, it would be Friends. It's a fun group of people that live in huge apartments and have seemingly endless free time on their hands. They very rarely work, yet always have enough money to do what they want. Wouldn't that be a nice life"?

DeniseW: "Seinfeld because it was such a great show. People's actual problems were laughed about making them seem not so insurmountable".

CHAPTER 14—ARE YOU PREPARED FOR MENOPAUSE? HAVE YOU HAD ANY PERIMENOPAUSAL SYMPTOMS? HOW DOES THAT MAKE YOU FEEL?

The consensus here seems to be that the majority of us are just not thinking about menopause because we would rather not. The truth of the matter is that most women will begin to experience what they now term 'peri-menopausal' symptoms, about 10 years before actual menopause sets in. The problem with these 'peri' symptoms is that many of us do not know what they are and we are attributing them to just simple aging, when in fact it is a precursor of things to come. We have all noticed changes in our monthly cycles, fatigue, and more difficulty with PMS and slower metabolisms. These are all, technically at least 'peri' symptoms. And we fit the age profile too. The vast majority of women enter true menopause in the late forties to early fifties—hello ladies, that figures to be about 10 years from now. Again, society has made us fear menopause as we have feared the big 40. As something we should dread. Here again, this does not have to be the case. While it is true that many women suffer through horrible symptoms of menopause, hot flashes and irritability spring immediately to mind, it is also worth noting that we have many more options for dealing with these symptoms than our mothers did. We now have before us a host of HRT (hormone replacement therapy) both natural and synthetic. While there is controversy-surrounding HRT (as there is with most hormone therapies) there are also many benefits. We also have a whole series of holistic treatments that were not widely know when our Moms were going through "the change". We are also a generation of healthier, more exercise conscious women. All these things may help us to have an easier time with menopause, thus eliminating some of the anxiety that goes along with the symptoms. If you are experiencing any symptoms or have any questions, consult your OBGYN or other doctor for some sound medical advice. Don't be afraid to explore your options.

I think a big part of the fear of menopause for women is the end of our childbearing years. Even when we are sure we have had all the children that we intend to, the fact that it will become impossible is unnerving. Bearing the children, being the preservers of the race, giving the gift of life, man, we have held this over men's heads for centuries! Like they had absolutely nothing to do with getting that little bun in the oven! I think most women are proud of the fact that this has been our gift. Ever hear a women brag about how she made it through labor without an epidural? Or how she pushed for 6 hours. Our husbands could never do that! We are sure of it! Even Elena, who is pregnant with numbers five and six says that the thought of never being able to have another child makes her uncomfortable. It may be the fact that the 'choice' is gone from the equation. Even late in our 30s and early in our 40s, as long as menopause has not hit us, we still have the CHOICE whether or not to have a baby. Once menopause sets in, that choice is taken away from us. And we all know that women like to have our choices. BethL at 38 is still hoping to be a Mom, so menopause is a 'four letter' word to her. Some of us have a little different take. We are welcoming it. Confident in our decision not to have any more children, and so sick and tired of our periods, Tracy, Sophie, Nancy and I are all for it. Of course, we all want to breeze thought it too!

Since this is such a serious topic, I think we need a little levity here. I am going to go with Nancy answer as my favorite. When posed the question *"Are you prepared for menopause? Have you had any perimenopausal symptoms yet? How does that make you feel"?* Nancy responded: "Let me tell you, menopause can't be any worse than those God awful cramps we get every month"! I kind of feel the same way, so I guess that is why I enjoyed her response.

The rest of the ladies had this to say about menopause:

Judy: "Bring it on! My Mom had an easy menopause so I am hoping for the same. We do not plan on having any more children and I HATE my period these days. I am almost eager for menopause. I thought I was having some perimenopausal symptoms, but it turned out to symptoms of my Hypothyroidism, and is now more under control. This really pissed me off because I was in the middle of enjoying my 'sexual peak' and this all started happening and put an abrupt end to that"!

Evie: "Oh no! I am in denial on that one. I have had no symptoms so far, thank God".

Sophie: "I am definitely not prepared for menopause. I had hot flashes once and I was soooooooo uncomfortable, and it made me feel really old. I have avoided looking into HRT (hormone replacement therapy) because if I don't look I wont have to deal with it. Not the best strategy I am sure. If symptoms get to the point where I become too uncomfortable, I will check out what my options are. I certainly wont miss having my period every month. About 5 years ago I developed the desire to have another child. My husband has no children of his own, but I had my tubes tied after my son was born and would have had to under go in-vitro fertilization or a reverse tubal. In the end we decided that since the kids would be grown and gone in the next two years we would just sit back and wait for grandchildren".

Ellen: "Yes and no. I am not really sure what to expect so I do not give it much thought. Knowing me, I probably won't even know that I am embarking on menopause until it hits me over the head. My Mom seemed to have a hard time with it, starting in her late 40s, early 50's so I think I still have awhile".

Erin: "Haven't thought much about it at all".

DeniseB: "Probably not. I haven't had any symptoms yet".

BethL: "NO, I still want to be a mother! Once I have two children (if I am so blessed) then I will be ready. My cycle has not changed since my mid twenties, so I guess I am not having any symptoms".

Tracy: "Yes, I think I am prepared, but I am not looking forward to it. I have heard some real horror stories, but it is a part of life and I will just have to deal with it. I haven't had any symptoms yet".

Jenny: "I don't think any of us are really prepared for menopause. You just don't know how it is going to affect you. My sister, who is one year older than I am, is having a really hard time. She just had a partial hysterectomy and is still having problems. Am I going to go through the same thing in a year? I don't think there was anything she could have done to predict or prevent this. I think we just have to keep our fingers crossed and hope for the best".

Elena: "No, I haven't had any symptoms yet. But one side of me looks forward to a time of not worrying about birth control and the other part is saddened to think that I would no longer be capable of bearing a life. I am having numbers 5 and 6 in one month and do feel that my family will be complete. But the thought of menopause makes me feel old".

Priscilla: "Not sure how to prepare for it and no, no symptoms yet. My Mom breezed through menopause with no hot flashes so I can only hope the same for myself".

BethR: "I have not had any peri menopausal symptoms yet. I have had a few friends complain about them but for the most part they were people that are older than me so it hasn't really hit home yet. I only have one friend who is younger than me and was complaining about the start of hot flashes and I remember being shocked about it. So I doubt I am ready for this—whatever ready really means".

Nancy: "Let me tell you, menopause can't be any worse than those God awful cramps we get every month"!

Susan: "Is anyone really prepared for menopause? I don't think you can be. Although the idea of never having my period again and never having to look at another TAMPAX in my life is not necessarily a bad thing, I would have to guess that there is also a difficult emotional side that goes along with this. Menopause, more than turning 40 is a sure sign that we are getting older. I just can't think about menopause yet, because I still haven't had any children".

DeniseW: "I am not prepared. I just started to have symptoms like my cycle shortened from 28 to 24 days. That's really it. But I just cannot picture myself going through menopause. I am way too young, especially in my outlook".

CHAPTER 15—WHAT IS YOUR BIGGEST REGRET IN LIFE?

This is another very serious question. I am starting to feel like maybe I should have included more of the fun questions! Anyway, our responses ran the gamut here. We had some very different answers to this question. Hey, that's what makes the world go round right? If everyone had the same responses, this would be a very boring, very short book. There were a few areas that a few of the ladies responded similarly on. The first one I will get into is the children issue. BethR regrets that her family size couldn't be larger, and DeniseB regrets that she has not yet begun her family. I regret that a daughter is missing from my family mix. All the answers were about children, but in all different contexts. Evie and Sophie regret the dissolution of their marriages and all the implications that go along with being a divorced parent and raising kids. DeniseW feels that maybe she didn't handle her divorce the way she would have liked. Elena and Jenny have a very different kind of regret. They both went with the missed opportunity, the "what could have been" response. I think this type of regret haunts a lot of people. Our lives take such different directions based on what seems like the simplest decision; for instance, Elena mentions regretting not joining the Peace Corps and attempting to save the world. This made me feel absolutely horrible because I distinctly remember one drunken night when Elena had the application for the Peace Corps and Priscilla and I were trying to talk her out of it! I don't think either of us realized the far-reaching affects of this night. I apologize to Elena for doing this, but Priscilla and I just could not stand the thought of her being gone so long and being so far away. We were selfish, but we are still glad she hung around. I wonder if Priscilla even remembers that night? I wonder if Elena does? I have probably just dug up a can of worms. Sorry, but Elena's response just brought that night right back to me. Forgive me.

There were two responses that I just thought were great. In a sense BethL and Tracy sort of summed up the great thing about turning 40, or about aging in general. Both of them say their biggest regret is that they did not more self-confidence and self-respect when they were younger. I think these are such important issues, especially for women. In one-way or another, either by our families or society little girls are still primarily being brought up to be the "people pleasers" and the "keepers of the peace". Little boys are often taught to fight for what they want, we are taught to compromise. Even as mothers, wives and adult daughters we are constantly sacrificing our needs and wants in order to put our children, husbands, family and sometimes friends need first. Somewhere around the late 30s some of us, like BethL and Tracy, begin to take a different attitude. We no longer need or seek the approval of other people. As our children age we begin to do a few things that make us happy. We realize we have built amazing and difficult careers in a "man's world" as BethL has, and raised a happy, healthy family as Tracy has. These things bolster our egos. We realize we are worthwhile and necessary parts of society. We find our self-esteem and our self-respect. My God, 40 is good for us.

So choosing a favorite here was again difficult, but I am going with Tracy. When asked, *"What is your biggest regret in life"?* Tracy responded: "Not having the self-esteem that I have now, and doing the stupid things that go along with low self-esteem. Caring too much about what other people thought about me and if they liked me". It also helps to know Tracy here. She is absolutely a more confident and secure individual than she was in high school and college. She's come a long way, baby.

Here are our regrets:

Judy: "This was an easy question for me to answer. I probably have only one real regret and that is not having a daughter. There is a little whole in my heart that will never heal because of what is missing. My boys are more than precious to me and I would never want to trade them in for a girl. I would just loved to have had a girl in ADDITION to my boys. I have such a great relationship with my Mom and have always felt I would like to share this with a daughter of my own. It has taken me a long time to get used to the idea that this will never happen for me. We did not want to try for a third child since we only wanted a girl. It just didn't seem right. I want desperately to adopt but my husband is against it".

Evie: "My biggest regret is not working at my marriage harder while we still had the chance, and taking that relationship for granted—just expecting it would recover and always be there. My daughter's upbringing will be very different from mine in this respect and I regret that too".

Sophie: "My biggest regret in life was getting married for the wrong reasons and subsequently getting a divorce. I was sexually promiscuous because of the confusion caused by the abuse I suffered as a child. I have stressed to my daughter that although sex may feel good, it feels better and is more satisfying with someone you care for".

Ellen: "Not being married for a longer period of time before having our first child".

Erin: "My biggest regret is not having spent more time with my Mother and Brother before they died. At the time it seems almost impossible to do considering all your other obligations. But after a person is gone…What you wouldn't give for just one more day with them".

DeniseB: "My biggest regret is not having children when I could have".

BethL: "My biggest regret is that I didn't respect myself sooner. I made some pretty bad "low self-esteem" decisions early on (i.e. dated the wrong men, didn't ask for a raise or promotion). I didn't have enough confidence to do the things I really wanted to do".

Tracy: "Not having the self-esteem that I have now, and doing the stupid things that go along with low self-esteem. I spent too much time and energy caring too much about what other people think about me and if they liked me".

Jenny: "Nothing too tragic. I wish I had done a semester abroad while I was in college. A couple of guys I wish I had kissed. There are so many variables in life, that when I start wondering if things would be different or better if I had done things differently or had different experiences it makes my head spin. Besides, why are we talking about regrets? We're still young. If there is something you want to change, change it. The fat lady hasn't sung yet"!

Elena: "Regret is a hard feeling. There are many things in my life I would have liked to do that I know I won't but I would not give up anything I have now to go back and try something different. I chose to marry and have a family and can't imagine my life without my husband and children. I had dreamed of joining the Peace Corps. As a teen and saving the world. I also dreamed of going into the theatre and singing. These things won't be what I am remembered for but I try to incorporate them into my life. Local theatre, singing at weddings, running clothing and toy drives".

Priscilla: "That my Dad didn't live to get to know his grandchildren".

BethR: "My biggest regret will probably surprise you Jude…I regret not having more children. By the time I had recovered from having Emily and Jack and felt ready to have more, it seemed like it was too late. I had the obligatory miscarriage and the spacing of the kids got farther and farther apart. If I got pregnant easily, without fertility drugs, I would have had at least one more. Joe had been pushing for more since Jack & Emily were born so he would have been a willing participant. We even looked into adoption, but our financial situation changed and that was no longer a possibility. That will probably be the hardest thing to swallow about menopause—when there are real signs that the door is closed forever (to having children)". (Note from author—response did not surprise me one bit. I have known Beth for over 20 years. She doesn't give me enough credit!)

Nancy: "My biggest regret in life is that I didn't spend more time living in New York City and experiencing all it had to offer. I had just moved to NYC when I met Matt. Matt is not a big city person and once I met him it was over for me in the city, I wanted to be with him, and that meant living in the suburbs. I'll get back there again, even if it means dragging 2 kids, a stroller, diaper bags, snacks, etc…"

Susan: "I don't think I have a biggest regret. My only regrets are not having had the time to spend with some people who are no longer with us. My father died of cancer in 1993 when he was only 54. I regret not spending more time with him, I guess I thought he would be around forever".

DeniseW: "That I didn't handle my divorce correctly".

CHAPTER 16—HOW WOULD YOU LIKE TO BE REMEMBERED BY YOUR FAMILY AND FRIENDS?

Most people don't like to think about this question. Evie even gives me a slight reprimand by telling me that I am being 'morbid'. Maybe that's true, but it is a question to ponder. This seems like it should be simple, most people want to be remembered as good and kind, but we have dug just a little deeper to find out what is really important to us. It might be interesting to take mental notes here, one of the questions coming up a little later deals with those characteristics that you value in those people closest to you. I am just wondering if many of the responses will be the same? I guess what I am asking is do we value in others what we value in ourselves? Oooooh, I like that. I think that is a good observation on my part. I really just thought of this just now. If you could see the silly grin on my face you would all be laughing. I will try and make note when we get to that question, because I have definitely aroused my own curiosity, and hopefully yours. A few of us listed 'a person you can count on' as one of the ways we would like to be remembered, a level head in a tough situation. I think these are both qualities that many people find difficult to live up to. Think for a minute of how many people you know that you can absolutely count on, no matter what? There are probably only a few, right? If you have more than a few consider yourself extraordinarily lucky! What about a friend or family member who can always keep a level head even in an emergency situation? How many people like this do you truly know? Don't most people we know freak out at the sight of blood? Or turn off the news because it has become too difficult to handle? I would be willing to bet that BethL doesn't do that. I think I would want her on my side of a tough situation. I think she could be my level head. Just so I am not making myself sound wimpy here, I am a great person to have in a tough situation, as long as it is *your* tough situation and not mine. I have dislodged food and candy from the mouths of several of my friends choking children, while remaining the only calm person in the room (BethR taught me the proper steps to take, she is a Pediatric Nurse). I don't know how I would be if it were my child. Anyway, all these things are important. Almost all the girls went with the obvious, good wife, mother, daughter, friend, I mean who would want to be remembered as *bad* at any of these roles? Some of the other adjectives included; trustworthy and compassionate, loyal, and a good sense of humor. One of the girls took it so far as to just say "happy". You will have to read on to find out the identity of that woman. From everything I have read prior to this question (and remember I have the added advantage of knowing everyone's responses to the latter ones) I feel confident in saying that these women will be remembered just the way they have chosen. I honestly can't think of one really negative thing to say about any of them, other than some of them made me *badger* them mercilessly just to get their responses back! I do go on don't I?

OK, this is going to be tough, choosing a favorite response. Once again I really like them all. I am not always sure exactly why I choose one and not one of the others; sometimes something about one just gets to me. That was the case here. I liked Nancy's response to this question. It was simple and right to the point. When asked, **"How would you like to be remembered by your family and friends"?** Nancy says: "I want to be remembered as someone who always tried her best to be the best mother, wife, daughter, friend and colleague that I could be and that I always tried to see the best in others". I can attest to the fact that Nancy does in fact always see the best in others.

Now let's take a look at our morbid epitaphs, if you will:

Judy: "Boy did I have trouble with this one. I had to come back to it. I think I would like to be remembered as a person you could count on. If I could be remembered as a good mother, wife, daughter and friend then that would be the greatest compliment of all".

Evie: "Morbid question Jude! The answer is a simple one 'happy'.

Sophie: "I would most like to be remembered as someone who cared about people and was a good listener and a good friend. I don't really care if people like me or not, because there are certainly people that I don't like! I would like to be seen as someone who gets along with all different kinds of folks".

Ellen: "As someone who did not fail anyone, especially my husband and children. In doing so I guess that would mean that I always did everything I possibly could for them. I would like to be remembered as honest, selfless and as a person who cared deeply for my family and for others. That I was someone that you could always count on".

Erin: "I would like my family and friends to remember me as a good, kind person. I try to live each day being decent to all people that I encounter. I know that I don't go out of my way with grandiose gestures, but I do try to be kind, or at least patient, to everyone I meet".

BethL: "I would like to be remembered for my sense of humor. As a person who was always there for you when you needed a level head in a sticky situation. I want to be remembered as a caring and thoughtful person".

DeniseB: "I just want to be remembered as a person who was good to others and to myself, as someone who did not say bad things about people and was an honest person".

Tracy: "As a caring and thoughtful person. Someone you could always count on".

Jenny: "I would like to be remembered as loving, caring, compassionate, kind, good and fun".

Elena: "I would like to be remembered as a good mother, wife and person who put my family and friends first while helping as many other people along the way as I could".

Priscilla: "As a caring, generous and good natured person with a good sense of humor who put tremendous value on her role as mother and friend".

BethR: "I would like to be remembered as a good friend and a caring person (maybe not so good at keeping in touch Jude, but you know I still love you!) I hope people remember me as being loyal and trustworthy".

Nancy: "I want to be remembered as someone who always tried her best to be the best mother, wife, daughter, friend and colleague that I could be and that I always tried to see the best in others".

Susan: "I would like to be remembered as a fun, caring, loving person, as someone who was there when they were needed, as a person who made a difference in people's lives no matter how small that difference may be".

DeniseW: "I want to be remembered as a loving mother, a great wife and a loyal friend".

CHAPTER 17—ARE YOU TURNING INTO YOUR MOTHER? IS THAT GOOD OR BAD?

I admit to secretly loving this question. I sort of giggle every time I read it. As a teenager what did we all complain about? Our mothers, and boys. Who did we all swear we would never be like? OUR MOTHERS! Well guess what? Seems like this might have happened despite all our years of trying to be just the opposite. This is a little bit frightening for several reasons. First of all, does this mean that we are old? Does it mean we are gong to be *exactly* like our Mothers? Does it mean our poor children will have to listen to endless anecdotes about our childhoods? Will we torture them with pathetic stories of how we had such rough childhoods and how lucky they are? Will we ever utter the words "there are children starving in Africa you know, so eat"! You better believe we will! Some of us feel that we can already hear our mother's words just slipping out of our mouth. I think we have all had that experience more times than we care to count. Ever hear yourself saying "because I'm the Mom that's why" or "no swimming for a half hour after lunch" (which by the way has no basis in medical fact). And so we begin the slow process, it actually takes years, of becoming our mothers. A few of the victims, like Sophie and Priscilla do not find this to be true. For the rest of us it almost seemed and inevitability. Remember question # 11 "who has had the biggest influence on your life?" Well, Tracy, Elena and I all said our Mom's specifically, had the biggest influence on our lives, while Ellen, DeniseB and Jenny said both parents which Mom is one half of. It seems to make perfect sense for us to become them in one way or another. Our parents are the people we learn to 'parent' from, whether this is good or bad can be up to us. We can choose those things we thought our Mother's did well, maybe your mom was a good, stern yet loving disciplinarian, maybe she was a great listener and confidant, maybe she always made you feel special and loved. Maybe she has a specific talent that you want to emulate, maybe she was musical or was a great cook and loved entertaining, maybe she always made your friends feel welcome, maybe she was a great painter like Jenny's Mom, or a had an eye for fashion and decorating. Since we all know that no person is perfect it is up to us to take what we feel is the best of our Mothers and use it. Just as we have the ability to choose which positive qualities to emulate we can also choose which qualities do not serve us well (ok, I just saw the eyebrows of 15 Moms crinkle up in disbelief!), For instance Sophie and BethL mention that their mothers grew up in a different time and had very different experiences and therefor are a more "close-minded' than Sophie and BethL would like to be. Both women have made a conscious effort to be more open-minded than they believe their moms to be. Once again, a valuable learning experience. Remember it is as important to know what you *don't* want as it is to know what you *do* want. Live and learn. And in Nancy's case she just feels that though she and her mom do have a lot in common, they are two very different people with very different qualities, so turning into her Mom is probably not likely for Nancy.

For favorite response here I would like to go with Elena. When asked the question *"Are you turning into your Mother? Is that good or bad?"* Elena says: "Oh yes! I laugh when I hear some of my mother's words coming out of my mouth! Since she is one of the people who I value most in life I am okay with this. I try to emulate her good qualities and laugh at myself when I say and do things that she did that drove me crazy as a kid".

I think I like it because Elena tries to take what she sees as her mother's positive qualities and incorporate them into her own, she is also able to laugh at herself when she sees herself as her mother.

Here is the way the rest of us are rationalizing turning into our Mothers:

Judy: "In some way I am definitely becoming my Mom. I have carefully chosen those things about my Mom that I think are great and I work at being like her. My mom is a survivor and one of the strongest people I know. She was widowed at 37 and has had open-heart surgery twice, yet I have never heard her utter a single complaint. I think I have done well on 2 out of 3 of these qualities. I tend to complain a bit, but am working on doing it less. I really have so much to be thankful for. My mother was also VERY strict, although to this day I am not sure she sees it that way. Growing up I swore I would NEVER be like this. I would be the kind of parent who is more of a friend to their child. Not happening. Our children are not given free reign. We are their parents, not their friends. A friend implies equality in a relationship. The parent-child relationship is not an equal one. I think my mom knew this years ago. My Mom was always big on affection and I always felt very safe and loved. I try and recreate that environment for my boys and I think I do a good job here. Despite the loss of my Dad at such an early age (I was 9) I had a very happy childhood. My Mom also had the good sense to marry a good, loving caring man who has always been a wonderful father to me. In many ways I did just as she did when I married Michael, a good, loving caring man who is a wonderful father (and like Tom in some ways)"

Evie: "HAHAHAHAHAHAHAHA! It scares me, some of the things that come out of my mouth when I am talking to Cecelia. And that's not good. No offense Mom. I have actually been doing a lot of reading to learn alternative methods of dealing with situations, other than my automatic reflex response. It's hard to unlearn what is ingrained in you since childhood".

Sophie: "The worst insult would be to say I am like my Mother. I think of her as a very rigid and close-minded person. She admits to these things, but at the same time I see her as more relaxed than she used to be. I do know that she has always done the best she could for me. In that way I guess I admire her. I just wish that she would have been more open to asking others for help or guidance when difficulties struck our family".

Ellen: "Yes, sometimes it's good, because like my mother, if it weren't for me, we wouldn't do anything around here. I am the initiator of everything (sound a little resentful don't I?) I have become more controlling like her, which at times is not good. I would do anything for anyone when asked, which can really stretch me to my limits and make me cranky with my family. She was sometimes and still is bitchy and I can be too. That can be very bad. Because I did not like that growing up and I hate that I can be like that now. I am much more affectionate towards my children than she ever was. I did always know that she loved me".

Erin: "Yes I think I am very much like my Mother. We are both very quiet people who keep our struggles to ourselves. My Mom was in so much pain and her life was so hard toward the end yet she never complained. She always asked about my kids and was more concerned about their health than her own. I don't think I'm there yet in that respect but it is something I admire about her".

DeniseB: "I know that I already have a lot of my Mother's traits, but I don't think I am turning into her. I am probably more like my father, quiet and subdued. If I do turn into my mother at some point, I would view it as a good thing".

BethL: "I am definitely more adventurous than my mother. There are certainly things about her that I would love to pass on to the next generation. But I don't ever want to be close-minded. The Army has introduced me to so many other cultures and socio-economic backgrounds. These experiences I would like to add to my mother's work ethic and her faith".

Tracy: "Yes, I am turning into my mother! I think it is good. I think she is a warm and funny person who can laugh at herself".

Jenny: "For better or worse I have always been my Mother. We don't really look that much alike, but people say we do because our expressions and mannerisms are so similar. Our voices and manner of speaking are also alike, so people tend to get us confused on the phone. We have very similar outlooks and values. Sometimes it scares me though. My Mother has always done this thing where she hums, absent-mindedly. I always thought that this was nuts. Now, of course, I do the same thing. What can you do? I love my mother and I think she is a great woman. I am proud to be like her. I just want to modify it a bit. Now if only I could learn to paint like her..."

Elena: "Oh yes! I laugh when I hear some of my mother's words coming out of my mouth! Since she is one of the people who I value most in life I am okay with this. I try to emulate her good qualities and laugh at myself when I say and do things that she did that drove me crazy as a kid".

Priscilla: "No I am not turning into my mother and that is a good thing. My mom has become a bit cynical in her old age and I refuse to do that. I will always strive to see the cup as 'half full'".

BethR: "My dad and my husband, Joe, are always saying that I am turning into my mother. I don't think that it is a bad thing, but I also don't necessarily think it's true. On certain issues I would agree, but 'turning into' sound pretty all-inclusive and that just isn't the case. I happen to think she was a pretty great lady and there are certainly worse people that I could turn into so...I take it as a compliment".

Nancy: "I am the polar opposite of my mother. My Mom is quiet, calm, conservative and a homebody. I am hyper and cannot stand to be home for more than 5 minutes at a time. My husband, Matt, always tells me that I do not know how to relax, which is true. It's just that there is always something that has to be done or somewhere I feel that I have to go".

Susan: "Not being a mother myself yet, I don't think that I am turning into mine—YET! I believe we all turn into our mothers in one way or another. There have been times that I have said things and then thought to myself 'I sound just like my Mom'. A mother is a huge influence on a girl's life. You are bound to become somewhat like her, you just may not see it".

DeniseW: "Luckily I have only picked up some of the good traits from my mother like getting in touch with my ethnic background a little more (I am Italian), and keeping in touch with family and friends. What I have not picked up, and never will, is that 'guilt factor.'"

CHAPTER 18—DO YOU CONSIDER YOURSELF A LUCKY PERSON?

To the ladies interviewed there are two words that seem interchangeable when speaking of luck, "lucky" and "blessed". Not that I'm counting (which I do for every question) but everyone but *one*, and that is 13 women, all consider themselves lucky, very lucky, or even blessed. BethR can't seem to decide, she begins by saying she is not exactly "unlucky" and finishes up with saying that she is lucky when it comes to the important, life altering stuff, so I wasn't exactly sure where to classify her. I'll give her her own special, confused, classification. Let's talk about the one person who doesn't consider herself lucky. Now you have to remember that each question is open to individual interpretation. Some people may consider luck simply to be things like winning the lottery. While other people may consider it on a much grander scale "I have my health, therefore I am lucky". And isn't it difference that makes the world go round? Jenny seems to belong to the first group, even referring to herself as unlucky (just a little superstitious). Even so, she feels that since luck, or lack thereof, has never been with her that this has made her even more "self determined". I think that is excellent. Once again one of my girls is taking a bad, or unlucky as context would have it, situation and walking away with a valuable, positive lesson. As for the rest of us 14 *"lucky"* ones we had a slew of reasons for believing ourselves lucky. Worth mentioning is that six of us, Priscilla, Tracy, Erin, BethL, Sophie and myself all used the word "blessed" or "blessings" when referring to luck. We all refer to mainly the same reasons for feeling "lucky" or "blessed" our health and our families. Sophie even mentions that she feels blessed because of a close call at age 10 when she was almost electrocuted! Erin likes to look around her at other people and see what they are dealing with and then counts her own "blessings". I think everyone should do this. In most cases, and there are always exceptions, when you feel like you have just been dealt more than you can handle, look around you, at your husband, your children, your family and your friends, do a quick summation and then "count your blessings". I think Oprah had suggested something like this a few years back on her TV show. I believe she called it a "Grateful Journal" or something along those lines. In this journal, everyday, you were to write down at least one thing you were grateful for. It could be simple, like, "I am grateful that it didn't rain on my child's birthday party" to something much more far reaching, like "I am grateful that my mammogram came back fine". Most of us probably don't have the discipline to sit down everyday and do this, but if we make an effort now and then some of those people who feel they are in the "unlucky" group may join us in the "lucky" one.

As far as my favorite response is concerned I really liked what Evie had to say. When asked, ***"Do you consider yourself a lucky person?"*** Evie responded: "I used to believe that if I were a gorgeous, thin, popular, rich, famous person then I would be lucky and that anyone who fit that description was lucky. But my idea of what luck is has changed, and I believe people who achieve their goals with hard work and love are the lucky ones. You have to work at being lucky, so I guess you could say I am working on it".

I like this response so much because I think so many people feel this way. I mean those thin, gorgeous, famous, rich people sure do look happy don't they? It may be easier at times to believe that luck is what got them there when in fact it could be a combination of hard work and a ton of plastic surgery. This also refers back to one of the previous questions (funny how this keeps happening—do you think it's on purpose?) #6—"if you could be anyone dead or alive, who would it be?" Everyone has their "unlucky" moments, some people just do a better job dealing with, or disguising them. I also liked what Evie said about "working on" her luck. I also believe this to be true; to a certain degree you can make your own luck.

Let's see what the rest of the girls said:

Judy: "I never used to consider myself lucky. It's funny how having kids changed all that. I grew up believing that God had a personal vendetta for me (I am 100% Italian and we do believe in vendetta!). I considered myself unlucky. Bad things just used to happen to me. My attitude changed when Tommy was born. I suddenly felt like the luckiest, most blessed person alive, and let me tell you a little change of attitude goes a long way".

Evie: "I used to believe that if I were a gorgeous, thin, popular, rich, famous person the I would be lucky and that anyone who fit that description was lucky. But my idea of what luck is has changed, and I believe people who achieve their goals with hard work and love are the lucky ones. You have to work at being lucky, so I guess you could say I am working on it".

Sophie: "I consider myself blessed, if you want to call that lucky. I was almost electrocuted at age 10 while trying to pull a plug out of the wall with a pair of scissors. I have been careless with regards to my sexual behavior, but besides an unexpected pregnancy, never suffered from any terrible diseases. Despite the fact that I was sexually abused I have learned to trust others, to be committed to one man, to love God and to love my children. I have been especially blessed to have two children who I can kid around with but who both recognize that I am their mother first and their friend second. I believe that the sexual abuse I suffered made me more aware of other people's feelings and made me more understanding and sympathetic".

Ellen: "How can I not feel lucky? I have my health, a wonderful husband and three beautiful children. After 9/11 shouldn't we all consider ourselves pretty lucky"?

Erin: "Yes, I am lucky. I have been given so much, my children, Frank. My life is good! I see the difficulties that other people have and I count my blessings".

DeniseB: "I would say I am lucky, I have my health and my family".

BethL: "Some would call it luck, other blessings. I would call it both. I am a faith-filled person. I believe that I have a say in my own destiny. God has blessed me with many gifts. I have used them to the best of my ability. I have tried not to waste them. I surround myself with good people and many good things have happened in my life".

Tracy: "I consider myself blessed. God has given me a family and a comfortable life and although there have been stressful times we have always pulled through".

Jenny: "No, I have bad luck. I don't know why. Whenever I spill salt I throw it over my left shoulder, just to cover myself. I always give the 'malocchia' whenever someone says something bad, and I still have bad luck. It stinks. That is why I've been forced to put more faith in self-determination. Luck never seems to work out for me".

Elena: "I am one of the luckiest people I know. My entire life luck has been with me. Even when I did not get something I wanted it has most often turned out to be for the best. I am so grateful for this".

Priscilla: "Absolutely! I have been blessed with a terrific family and a huge circle of friends. They have all brought me enormous happiness in my life and I will always be thankful for this".

BethR: "I don't really think of myself as 'lucky'. I really think people, for the most part, make their own luck by preparing or not preparing for situations. If you mean luck, in terms of winning lotteries or prizes, well I never do, but then again I don't even enter so it could be argued that I am making my own 'lack of luck' by not participating. I am lucky in terms of the shitty little things that can happen to people that are in no way influenced by their behavior i.e.; what family you are born into, health problems, death of loved ones, natural disasters etc".

Nancy: "I always try and remind myself that I am the luckiest person in the world. First of all I was lucky enough to be born to two very generous and loving parents who gave me the opportunity to see the world and have faith in me not to make the wrong decisions. Now I am extremely blessed with two fantastic (albeit totally opposite) loving boys who give me all the joy in the world. All I have to do is look into their innocent, wonderful faces to know how lucky I am to know such an unconditional love".

Susan: "I guess I do consider myself a lucky person. I am lucky that I grew up in a good family, I have great friends, and I have a job that supports me. I have a place to live, food to eat, a car to drive and money to spend on the things I enjoy. I have my health and I am educated. A lot of people don't have these things. I have not had everything in my life go my way and I don't have everything that I want from life, but yes, I do consider myself lucky".

DeniseW: "I do consider myself lucky. I have a beautiful daughter, Sierra, a wonderful husband in Alan, a beautiful home and a great career. I am extremely lucky".

CHAPTER 19—HOW IS YOUR RELATIONSHIP WITH GOD? HAS THIS CHANGED SINCE YOUR TWENTIES AND THIRTIES?

Well, God should be very happy with the news here. It seems in our "old age" that many of us are turning back to the church and more specifically to God Himself (or Herself whatever you choose to believe). For most of us it seemed that in our 20s and maybe even our early 30's were the pretty selfish, heathen years. We didn't really go to church and if we did it was out of a sense of obligation, (or in Elena's case because a cute guy was there) not because we enjoyed it or truly wanted to be there to praise God. We all sort of put God on the back burner for a while and went about living our hedonistic lives and not thinking too much about God. And MANY of us went to Catholic college, need I remind you of the number of Siena girls that have participated in this book! Evie, Elena, BethL, DeniseW and Jenny all attended Catholic high schools. We should be ashamed of ourselves! Jenny even refers to herself as a "nice Catholic girl". By the way, does anyone know a nice boy we could fix a "nice Catholic girl" up with? She is Italian and a good cook. Send all inquiries to me please. Include photo. Sorry, rambling again. Anyway back to the topic at hand. God. It's funny how we ALL mention coming back to God within the past several years. Is it age that brings us closer to God, or the inevitable dealing with our own mortality? Is it children? That seems to be the case for many of us. Ellen and Nancy write that they rely more on their faith since the birth of their children than they ever did before. DeniseW feels that she really didn't have a relationship with God early on, but does now. Let me ask all the parents out there, how many of you have screamed, either out loud or to yourself "God, give me patience!!!!" Elena's faith was reaffirmed when she recently began teaching a CCD class. Probably the fact that she married the cute guy from church and is now expecting their 5th and 6th child with him didn't hurt either. Boy, she really does have God to thank for Joe! For BethL, who also experienced a deepening in her faith recently, it was her husband's decision to convert to Catholicism. For myself, the rediscovery of my faith later in my life has changed my life immeasurably. I truly wish I had done so years ago and I don't honestly know why I didn't. I think most people find it comforting to have someone to lean on, someone who they know will always be there, even if we have neglected them for many, many years, someone who is waiting, with open arms and no remandments to welcome us home.

Back to that old "favorite response". For this question I am going to have to go with myself again, little egomaniac that I am. I just think that I have come such a long way from believing that God actually did not like me, to knowing that He loves me. I know this was a long and difficult journey for me, but worthwhile in ways I never imagined. Here is my response. When asked, ***"How is your relationship with God? Has this changed since your twenties or early thirties?"*** Egomaniac and author, I replied: "This kind of goes back to the previous question for me. About 3 years ago I decided I needed some good old fashion faith in my life. I began by going back to church and by praying more. I began thanking God for every little thing, even finding lost keys. I no longer feel that God doesn't like me. I know that God loves me. I think our relationship is evolving. I love Church. I love to sing hymns and I love to sing loud even though I may not sing well! I pray everyday and count my blessings. I am not kidding I do this everyday. I no longer expect the worst outcome in every situation. I pray for strength to deal with whatever comes my way. We are definitely a work-in-progress, God and I".

Here's how the rest of the girls feel about their relationship with God:

Skip me because you just read it!

Evie: "I was raised in a staunch Irish Catholic household. We went to church every Sunday. I went to 16 years of Catholic school. There have been times when I have questioned my religion, but never my faith in God. I have actually been working on that aspect of my life too—trying to find a way to merge my own spirituality with my Catholic religion".

Sophie: "God was very important in my early years because I did not understand what was happening to me and why I felt so sad all the time (due to abuse). In my mid 20's I turned away from the church when the decisions I was making were not in line with the church's teachings. When I quit trying to rationalize my decisions to have relationships with married men, I turned back to my faith and have, as of my early 30's become more and more focused on studying my faith and understanding my reasons for believing or not believing".

Ellen: "I don't know how God feels, but I think our relationship is pretty good. Since I have had children I rely on my faith in God more and feel the need to provide my children with some kind of faith, which I can only do by example. Therefore, God and religion are very important aspects of my life. I believe that God truly gives us what he believes we are strong enough to handle in life. When bad things happened to me (in my early 20's) I did a lot of blaming on God. However, I made it through and have come out on the other side, still standing".

Erin: "I think my relationship with God is good. I just hope he feels the same way. I don't always give God as much of my time as I should but he is always there for me when I am ready to accept him.

God is the center of my life and from Him all things stem. God has always been important in my life. But I'm not sure if I always knew He was the most important part".

DeniseB: "My relationship with God is good. I probably pray more now than I did in my 20's or 30's".

BethL: "God has always been a part of my life. Sometimes his presence is more prevalent than others, my doing of course. My husband just recently converted to Catholicism. This act has deepened my faith. I am more aware of my blessings than I was in my 20s or 30s".

Tracy: "Getting better every day! I don't think I really had a relationship with God in my 20's. As I have gotten older and had children, faith has become very important. I am on my journey, as I like to call it, to find God everywhere and to build a close relationship with Him".

Jenny: "I have always been a nice Catholic girl, so my relationship with God has always been a part of my life. I think, as with my other relationships, it has strengthened and deepened, as I have gotten older. I take more comfort in it as time passes".

Elena: "My relationship with God has changed quite a bit over the years. In my 20's I went to church every week because the guy I had a crush on did. I wound up marrying him. In my early 30's I could take it or leave it because I was always too busy. When we started having kids we wanted them to be a part of the church. Late 30's has been an eye opener for me. I was asked to teach a religion class. Preparing for the class has really affirmed my faith and spirituality. I feel that spirituality on a whole new level now. I do not agree with everything the church teaches, but I am very comfortable with what I believe the church is teaching for me and my family."

Priscilla: "I think that everyone goes through periods where God may mean more to them. I am thankful that I have a strong faith and that my children have the same. Losing my Dad at such a young age was tough to take without my faith, I could not understand that there is more to life and we do need to go forward".

BethR: "My relationship with God is better now than previously. I became more religious after my Mom died, but I was leaning in that direction long before her death. I am not really sure what precipitated that".

Nancy: "My relationship with God has gotten closer now that I have children. I used to talk to God about selfish things for myself. Now I pray to God about making the world a safer and happier place for all children, and specifically about protecting my children and keeping them happy and healthy".

Susan: "I haven't been a church going person in many, many years. I go to church for funerals and weddings. On the other hand, I don't believe that you have to go to church to believe in God. Let's just say that I am not a good Catholic, but I would like to believe there is a God and that there is a better place, heaven, to go to in the next life. I would like to also believe that some of the trials we go through in life are really part of God's plan for us, and that someday when we get to heaven our questions will all be answered".

DeniseW: "I don't think I had a relationship with God early on. I went to Catholic grammar and high school so I rebelled a bit after that. I started a real realationship with God in my late 20's at which point I converted from Roman Catholic to Baptist. Since then, while I do not attend weekly services, God has been a very important part of my life and I speak with him every night before I fall asleep".

CHAPTER 20—WHAT ACTOR/MUSICIAN/POLITICIAN DO YOU FIND ATTRACTIVE? WHAT IS IT ABOUT HIM THAT YOU FIND SO APPEALING?

Time for more fun and games. This question is a total throwaway. I really just love to ask people, men and women, this question. Sometimes someone's answer really knocks your socks off. Like my quiet and shy friend, who was too young to participate in the interviews, whose response was "Denis Rodman" Oh my God I almost died! I thought for sure she would go with someone like Pierce Brosnan, who does get chosen by Nancy. I did love the responses to this question. We have several actors mentioned, scanning the generations from a young buff Matt Damon, to that perennial favorite Sean Connery. We even have a few politicians thrown in. I wont say who chose them or which politicians they are, but it ain't JFK! It's intriguing let me tell you, this was one response that surprised me! Jenny was so overwhelmed by the question that she couldn't even choose! BethR just can't seem to remember any particular names. There were no musicians represented here. That also surprised me. When we were younger, in our very early 20s, I know for a fact (Jenny can back me up here) that Jackson Browne and Bruce Springsteen would have appeared on this list. Ah, youth. How times change. Here is something to our credit, only Ellen in choosing Matt Damon, chose someone younger than the group! I think Evie's choice may be a few years our junior, but not too bad. The rest of us all chose MEN, our own age or even older. We chose Mel Gibson, Kurt Russell, Sean Connery, Pierce Brosnan, and perennial favorite, Robert Redford! No boy toys for us. We like our men "real" and "rugged". We like men of action and we like their buff bodies too. But we also like them to be close to our age so we feel like we have something in common with them. I feel almost certain, no I take that back, I *am* certain that if you posed this question to a group of 40 year old men the situation would be exactly reversed. There might be one or two men who chose a woman close to their age, say Christy Brinkley or Meg Ryan, but the remainder????? Halle Barry, Catherine Zeta Jones, Molly Simms. All gorgeous and talented woman, some just less chronologically advanced than others (that means young by the way).

So the ladies choose. I can't pick a favorite right now. I will have to come back. I'm back and I have to say these are all good responses. Notice there is only one duplicate here, and that is Mr. Robert Redford. So I will just congratulate all the lucky men who were chosen by these wonderful women and hope that they appreciate it.

Judy: "I adore Michael J. Fox. I have had a huge crush on him since before it was fashionable to do so. He has been making me laugh for 20 years, and I find that to be incredibly sexy. He is my longest relationship to date (though it is one sided)! For a while I lusted after David Duchovny, and still do a little. Right now my 'crush du jour' is Rob Lowe. He is one handsome man. But my crush to end all crushes is definitely Michael J. Fox".

Evie: "Uh, Noah Wylie (Dr. Carter on ER) Oh he is just so nice and cute and unassuming. He seems like a good guy".

Sophie: "I believe that I am struck positively by President Clinton. I have also liked President Nixon. I think that these two appeal to me because even though they made mistakes and got caught, they were able to continue to live their lives. We all make mistakes, although not quite as publicly as these gentlemen. Indiscretions, lies and the like are things I have dealt with but I still have to go on whether or not other people know".

Ellen: "It has changed over the years, but I would probably have to go with Matt Damon. I enjoy his boyish charm and good looks. I also think he is grateful for the life that he has become accustomed to and is humble in the presence of even the most regular people".

Erin: "Mel Gibson, cute as can be and doesn't seem to know it. Patrick Swayze, though I am not sure why, there is just something about him".

DeniseB: "Denzel Washington and Sean Connery, they seem very distinguished".

BethL: "Clint Eastwood, Keanu Reeves and Ed Harris. I just like man who knows he is a man—tough and smart. My husband looks like a younger Ed Harris". You lucky girl!

Tracy: "Tom Cruise still makes me smile. I think I like the whole package, excluding his personal life, of course".

Jenny: "Why do I have to pick just one? That's not fair. I don't have a certain physical type so there's a whole range of guys I think are gorgeous either because of the way they look or act or their personalities. I can't even list them. It would be pointless".

Elena: "I have always liked Robert Redford. He is attractive in a rugged sense without being too pretty. He has mostly chosen films that are meaningful. He has taken acting to a different level. He does not rely solely on his good looks. He also has not used the media to try and make himself into something he is not".

Priscilla: "I admire Harrison Ford because of his resolve to stick with the movie business. He was not discovered until his 30's and yet he is a true HUNK, even if he is dating that waif, Calista Flockhart. My younger brother is in the same profession and I hope that he too gets his big break someday".

BethR: "This is a bad question for me. I never remember the names of actors, musicians and the like, and I certainly don't think of them that way! I do see men in magazines and on TV that I think are hot, but it never seems to stick with me. I love guys with washboard abs and that seems to catch my attention".

Nancy: "I absolutely think George Clooney, Pierce Brosnan and Kurt Russell are hot, but why is it men get better looking with age? I like them because they are not only gorgeous, but they have a boyish way about them where they don't seem to take themselves too seriously. You can add Brad Pitt to that list too".

Susan: "I still think after all these years that Robert Redford is really hot! He is good looking in a rugged way. There is something so sexual about him, and those EYES! Put the man in a pair of jeans or a tux, whatever, he always looks good".

DeniseW: "Michael Douglas. Gorgeous, tough façade, successful and knows how to treat a lady."

CHAPTER 21—TELL ME SOME THINGS YOU DO JUST FOR YOU? DO YOU FEEL GUILTY ABOUT DOING THEM?

It seems like all of us get a chance to do something just for ourselves. What that is tends to differ depending on who you talk to. What is important here is that we are all trying to help ourselves. We are all pretty aware of the fact that if we are happier, calmer, more stable individuals that we will be better wives, mothers, daughters, and friends. It's really just a matter of finding out what works for you. If you are reading this and wondering what you can do 'just for you' I think you will excited to find a myriad of options here to choose from. Good luck and get busy!

Evie, BethR, Ellen, Erin and I all mentioned exercise as one of our guilty little pleasures. While BethL and Sophie did not mention this we now know that the good ole US Army keeps them exercising. This is a good response because it serves more than one purpose. First of all it helps keep us physically fit. This may seem like the obvious and most important benefit, but as BethR and Evie can attest, exercise has the power to calm and rejuvenate us, especially if you are practicing Yoga, Pilates or a similar technique that incorporates mind and body. Remember, you don't have to go to a fancy or expensive gym to exercise. Most local YMCAs offer fitness programs for all levels from beginner to the more advanced athlete. Walking and bicycle riding are two more excellent, low cost options that will work for just about anyone, even someone who has never exercised before. So stop making excuses and get out there and exercise!

For the vanity in us, a few of us mentioned manicures and/or pedicures. This is a very relaxing way to spend an hour or two and is relatively inexpensive if you avoid salons and spas, and instead opt for a chain. Tracy, BethL, Evie, Nancy and DeniseW and I all admit to indulging in this bit of tranquility, although Nancy can't seem to find it quite as relaxing as the rest of us. As I may have mentioned in a previous question, it is nice to have your nails and toes looking great even if you are feeling fat and are having a bad hair day. Representing the more cerebral part of us, Sophie enjoys puzzles while Jenny, Susan and DeniseB like to read. There were lots of other great activities mentioned, like planting flowers, shopping, and a good old-fashioned bubble bath. The thing that is important here is not "what" you do, it's that you do *something*. We all need a little get away, a private sanctuary were we feel totally indulgent. As we can see by the variety of answers here it doesn't even have to cost any money. A bubble bath, or a soak in the tub wont cost you anything. You can soak and read or listen to music or drink wine. You will come out feeling relaxed and you will even be clean!

A few ladies mentioned small, very small pangs of guilt, fortunately not enough to stop them from indulging in shopping, exercising, reading or what have you. Priscilla's response was interesting in that she was really the only one experiencing what she refers to as 'catholic guilt' at doing anything for herself! I really like the fact that she mentions that she experiences pleasure from helping others. This is probably why I have chosen Priscilla's response as my favorite one here.

When asked, ***"Tell me some things you do just for you? Do you feel guilty about doing them?"*** Priscilla responded: "Being Catholic, of course I feel guilty about doing anything remotely selfish. I keep it to a minimum. I enjoy, and take satisfaction from, taking care of others. I will drink a glass of wine on a work night and sit and read a magazine while the kids are watching TV. I get up early every morning, this is my 'clear your head time' and it is good for me. One of my favorite things is our Girl's Weekend. Each year my old college roommates and I get together and go away for a weekend. I never feel guilty about this. It is too much fun".

I would like to add here that I don't think this should be just a woman thing, or a 40-year-old thing. Everyone, husbands included need to be good to themselves. And if your man has trouble being good to himself, help him. Women are probably a little better at calling up the girls and moaning "I need a night out"! And like BethR says, we are ready in a moments notice. My God we go to Tupperware parties and to Pampered Chef things just to get out of the house! Most men don't have this. This is why they need things like golf and football pools and baseball things.

Here are the rest of out guilty little pleasures:

Judy: "Let's see, I get my nails done every 2-3 weeks. I may look a mess, but my nails *always* look good. I workout 4-5 times a week, that's for me mentally and physically. If I am particularly stressed I take a long, hot soak in the tubby. I can actually feel the stress and anxiety coming off me while I soak. I do an occasional "girls night out" with my friends now and then. Oh, and I am writing a book, perhaps I've mentioned that".

Evie: "I do Yoga and other exercises. I always feel great when I am there and long after it is over. There is absolutely no guilt there. I get pedicures once in a while. I love how it feels, but I feel badly for the person who had to do them! I enjoy store and catalog shopping. I end up returning a lot of it, so I guess there is some guilt involved there, unfortunately, not enough to stop me".

Sophie: "Things I do just for me are listening to books on tape, mostly mysteries, doing crossword and other puzzles or playing spider solitaire on the computer. I feel that the time on the computer is wasted (a little guilt) but the books on tape are a useful way to spend time in the car. Crosswords and puzzles help to keep my mind working, plus I can still hang out around my family while I "puzzle" away".

Ellen: "I go to the gym and I shop a lot. I belong to a book club and try to read a book once a month. I feel guilty when I shop but I love to do it. It makes me feel better when my home looks nice and my clothes look nice, but I do feel guilty about spending the money".

Erin: "Tennis is just for me, and yes, sometimes I feel a little guilty".

DeniseB: "I just hang out and read, go on vacations with friends or by myself. Sometimes I feel a little guilty".

BethL: "Manicures, pedicures and occasional bubble baths, and, oh yeah, chocolate. I do not feel guilty at all! I think little treats are what keep us going".

Tracy: "I get my nails done and hope to include an exercise program in the fall when the kids get back to school. No, I don't ever feel guilty".

Jenny: "This is a hard one—I mean, technically, I work just for me, so I can eat and pay the bills. Although, I guess I don't work solely for me. I have always worked in jobs that help people, or make things a little bit better. I don't think that what you're after here Jude. I read, take baths, listen to music. I plant flowers. I think it always feels better to do something for someone other than yourself, but that doesn't mean it is bad to do something just for you. We need to replenish. That's a good thing".

Elena: "I don't do a lot but I do get together with old friends who are women I used to teach with. We go out to dinner every few weeks. I don't feel guilty about it at all. My husband doesn't mind me spending some time with them and it gives me a chance to 'talk shop'. I know they value my opinions as a teacher and professional, and this boosts my confidence".

Priscilla: "Being Catholic, of course I feel guilty about doing anything remotely selfish. I keep it to a minimum. I enjoy, and take satisfaction from, taking care of others. I will drink a glass of wine on a work night and sit and read a magazine while the kids are watching TV. I get up early every morning, this is my 'clear your head time' and it is good for me. One of my favorite things is our Girls Weekend. Each year my old college roommates and I get together and go away for a weekend. I never feel guilty about this. It is too much fun".

BethR: "One thing I do just for me is exercise. It is a big priority in my life and I get cranky if I can't get to the gym. The only other thing I do just for me is my women's bowling league. I have been on a team for 4 or 5 years and it is 3 hours a week that I devote to just having fun and hanging out with the girls".

Nancy: "I get my nails done and my hair colored which you would think is relaxing, except that I am always thinking about what else I should be doing instead of sitting there wasting my time primping. The one fun thing that I do is make sure that I get together with my girlfriends once in a blue moon for a girl's night out or a long weekend. That is what keep's me sane".

Susan: "Not having anyone else to worry about but myself these days, I guess everything I do is just for me. And no, I do not feel guilty about that! I work really long hours; Sunday is usually my only day of total rest. I sleep late, lie on the couch and do crossword puzzles or read a book. I like to read and I also like to bake. I find both tasks to be very relaxing. I get enjoyment out of baking and sharing the goodies with others".

DeniseW: "I spend quite a bit of money on my hair. That's really about it. No, I don't feel guilty about it. Most everything else I do is for everyone else".

CHAPTER 22—WHEN WAS THE LAST TIME, IF EVER, YOU HAVE GONE AWAY WITHOUT YOUR HUSBAND AND KIDS? HOW DID THEY SURVIVE WITHOUT YOU? DID YOU HAVE A GOOD TIME?

Let me tell you, there are a lot of 'girls weekends' and 'girls night out' going on in this group. Actually not a lot, or what I mean is not really often, but we are getting around to it. Over the years what we have generally heard is the term 'male bonding' in reference to things that men enjoy doing together, like golf outings, sports events, paint ball whatever, and of course this is important. We females also need our bonding rituals, though ours tend to be centered on different activities. Almost everyone one of us has gone away for at least one weekend without her spouse and/or children. I really don't think I can stress the importance of this enough. I live for my once a year, long weekend with Ellen, Evie, Jenny, Erin and our other friend, Nancy. I love that my husband encourages me go with hardly any fanfare. I love the time I spend with these women. I *need* it. I think we all *need* some girl time. It is our little escape back to those carefree, college days when we had plenty of free time, little responsibility and little money. Only now we can enjoy our weekend getaway and we have some money to spend! We do ridiculous "girl" things. On our first excursion to Ft. Myers, Ellen did a Mary Kay demonstration on all of us. We drank lots of wine and made ourselves up with all the sample make-up, we laughed, and we had fun. I think it is safe to assume that our husbands would not ever want to be included in this activity. We went shopping (another activity most men find boring, and most women enjoy). We sat at the pool and the beach and reminisced and ate and drank. We took lots of pictures and acted silly. We were 6 college roommates again, carefree and energetic, if just for the weekend. It seems that the other Siena girls have pretty much the same ritual, a once a year, long weekend with the girls. Tracy and DeniseB both went away this year with our group of, what we call "high school" friends. This weekend was specifically designed to celebrate our 40th birthdays. We didn't have cake or a party, we didn't even really talk about turning 40, we just decided we would like to be together, without the added demands of husbands, kids, cooking or cleaning. We stayed at a mutual friends' vacation home in Connecticut and had a very nice weekend. Another group that gets away every year includes Elena, Priscilla and Susan. Only Elena refers to it specifically, Priscilla and Susan also attend. The word 'rejuvenate' comes up when referring to these weekends, and that is exactly what they do. For many of us it is really the only time all year that we are putting our needs and desires before everyone else's. It just plain feels good. Sophie even tells us that she has gone away by herself. She was just feeling that she needed a break and some time alone, so off she went. We are all lucky enough to have husbands and families who support our *need* to do this now and again. From what all the girls say, the husbands and children didn't seem to suffer too much while we wives and mommies took a short vacation. When you think about it, it is a great way for the Dads to get a little sampling of what life is like in the Mommy lane. They get to spend a little more time with the kids, without Mom around to say, "No, we don't do it that way". If there are no children on the scene yet, as in BethL case, this can be a good time for your husband to reconnect with his buddies a bit. Anyway, everyone seems to survive just fine without us and that is good for everyone. I'll let you in on a little secret, when we do our "Siena girls" weekend all we talk about is how wonderful our husbands are. Seriously, we are so thrilled with the fact that they don't mind our yearly excursion that we gush about them, where normally we might be more inclined to bitch a bit. It's so funny, it's like we are different women! I know that my neighbors have told me that while I am away Michael has been know to say "I don't know how she does it. I couldn't handle this day in and day out". Of course he doesn't say this to *me*, but the very fact that he feels it is enough for me.

We all come back from our little get away feeling refreshed, and yes, rejuvenated. We have wonderful memories, and immediately begin planning for next year. I would also like to make a special 'Thank You' here to Ellen's parents, Leo and Marilyn McCarthy, for being such wonderful, good sports and allowing 6 desperate ladies to descend on their Ft. Myers condo every year. We couldn't do this without their generosity and kindness. Thank you a million times over.

Some of us also have to travel for work, and this is a whole different ball game. Priscilla, Nancy and DeniseW all have careers that require them to be away from their families at times. This can be added stress, it is not usually a fun trip, you have to prepare work to take with you and you have to work while you are there. There is not relaxing or rejuvenating involved. As DeniseW says, she is generally anxious to get home after a few days.

So back to that favorite response thing. I think I have to go with Sophie on this one. When asked*: "When was the last time, if ever, you have gone away without your husband and kids? How did they survive without you? Did you have a good time"?* She responded: "Last year I was feeling overwhelmed with work and I had a long weekend coming up. I took a two-day vacation by myself at the beach before the season officially started. I walked by myself, slept by myself and ate by myself and it was so freeing! My husband did not understand my need to get away, but said that if I needed to go I should. The kids are old enough so it was ok with them. I think they understand that my moods are not necessarily to be understood, but just gotten through".

What I love about Sophie's response is that she realized she was feeling overwhelmed and that she needed some time to herself. Instead of moping around and making *everyone* miserable she chose to take action and resolve the problem. She went away, by herself, which I believe takes tremendous courage and found it freeing! Excellent! I hope she does this again.

Here are some of the things the rest of us like to do, just for ourselves:

Judy: "I went away with Tracy and DeniseB and a few other friends in June 2002 so we could all sort of celebrate our 40th birthdays. For the past 3 years I have also gone away with Evie, Ellen, Jenny, Erin and our other friend Nancy P for our now annual 'Girls' weekend'. Michael and the boys do just fine without mommy. They eat fast food and go to the arcade. I find my 'girls weekend' to be relaxing, rejuvenating and very necessary. I love my girls. We have the best time together. I also encourage my husband to get away with his golf buddies about once a year, and he and I try to get away for a long weekend alone each summer—thank you Mom and Tom for watching the kids! I think everyone needs alone time, Mommies, Daddies, kids, couples. It should be a given".

Evie: "Our 'girls' weekend' in Newport last October 2001! My daughter survived fine with good instructions and YES I had a fabulous time. There is nothing like a 'girls' weekend' to rejuvenate the soul. Laughter is very good for your health"!

Sophie: "Last year I was feeling overwhelmed with work and I had a long weekend coming up. I took a two-day vacation by myself at the beach before the season officially started. I walked by myself, slept by myself and ate by myself and it was so freeing! My husband did not understand my need to get away, but said that if I needed to go I should. The kids are old enough so it was ok with them. I think they understand that my moods are not necessarily to be understood, but just gotten through".

Ellen: "In Newport in October 2001 with Evie, Jenny, Judy, Nancy and Erin. My family survived just fine. Bob really picks up the slack when I am gone and I have all the confidence in the world that the kids are in good hands".

Erin: "In October 2001 in Newport, RI with a *wonderful* group of girl friends (can you guess who?). Yes, my family survived just fine".

DeniseB: "Does not apply".

BethL: "My husband and I both travel for business reasons. Often I mix business with pleasure. My husband was a bachelor since he was 18 so he is very self-sufficient. When we are apart we stay in touch daily by phone. If you can't have a good time you might as well be six feet under. You get only one shot at this life, make it your best".

Tracy: "In the spring of 2002 with my high-school girlfriends (Judy and DeniseB included) to celebrate our 40th birthdays. My family did just fine without me and I had a good time too".

Jenny: "Doesn't apply".

Elena: "I do one weekend a year with a group of my friends. My family always survives just fine! I do over prepare before I leave. I always look forward to my 'girls weekend' but I tend to feel a bit apprehensive before I leave. Once I am there I thoroughly enjoy myself. I am always ready to come home on Sunday morning".

Priscilla: "I often travel for work so I am away on a fairly regular basis. The kids are used to it and so am I. It only rarely becomes a problem. Right now, I am sitting in an airport on my way to Florida to be with my mom for some surgery tomorrow morning. My son, Parker, is sitting beside me and it is close to the anniversary of 9/11, so I guess that is why he seems to be sad on this trip".

BethR: "I have never been away on a pleasure trip without Joe and the kids. It has usually been for an emergency like my nephew Tommy's hospitalizations for Leukemia or my mother's illness and subsequent death. I did go to the PTA convention about 2 years ago but that had no fun involved! It was torture! I have a friend who gets away with the girls every year but she has never invited ME to go (I get the distinct impression that Beth is talking about me here. She knows damn well that I go with college friends that she doesn't even know). My friends and I have all threatened to do this but it never seems to happen. If the opportunity ever arises I will be there in a moment. I think time away from your job can only make you a better wife and mother. That is why I maintain my exercise schedule even when things get crazy at home. I find even a short break gives me more patience. Anytime I am away my family survives just fine. My friends and neighbors have always been there to help out and Joe is very capable".

Nancy: "I have to travel for my job, and so frequently have to leave my husband and kids home alone. Let's see, I make sure everything is spelled out with lists of their activities and homework and music lessons and practices. I pack their lunch money everyday and label it with the day of the week that it is for. So far they have all survived, but I wouldn't say the same thing about the house. I don't even want to go there"!

Susan: "Another one that I can't really answer".

DeniseW: "I travel for my job about 6 times a year. I am actually leaving next week for Las Vegas. My daughter stays with her father, but always knows that I am within arms reach. She gets sad, but we talk on the phone every night. My husband gets to watch his TV programs without hearing me bitch about it. He likes The History Channel. If the trip is more than 4 days, then everyone gets a bit more anxious for me to get home, myself included."

CHAPTER 23—DO YOU THINK ABOUT YOUR OWN MORTALITY? HAS THIS CHANGED SINCE SEPTEMBER 11TH?

I have decided to skip ahead today and do my responses out of sequence. See, today is September 11, 2002—exactly one year to the day of the great tragedy and loss we Americans suffered at the World Trade Center, the Pentagon and the plane crash in Pennsylvania. So many of the ladies I interviewed were affected by the events of 9/11. DeniseW was working in the city at BBDO when it happened. As mentioned earlier, Susan lost her beloved brother-in-law, Chris, a fact that changed her life and her outlook dramatically. Tracy, DeniseB and I were all raised in Rockville Centre, NY a mere 30-minute train ride into Manhattan. All of us knew several people lost in the World Trade Towers. RVC has the unfortunate distinction of being one of the towns hardest hit. It is impossible to say the events of this day have not forever changed us. In a way we lost our innocence that day, that feeling that, as Americans, we were impervious and impenetrable. I think it made a lot of people believers in fate. A few of the girls mentioned, "When your numbers' up it's up". We all know stories of people who didn't make it to the Trade Center that day for one reason or another. My friend Lucille usually goes into lower Manhattan every Tuesday via the WTC, on this particular day, even though her babysitter was willing, she was just too tired. Her lethargy may very well be the reason she is at home with her husband and children today. Another friend's brother was on the last train out of the WTC; he too was one of the lucky ones. And the stories, sadly work in reverse. The woman who was 8 months pregnant and due to take maternity leave, the gentleman who started his first day on the job at Windows on the World, and the extraordinarily brave members of the NYFD and NYPD who risked their own lives in order to save others. The people who missed their plane or changed their reservation at the last moment in a vein attempt to return to their families. And of course, the brave men on board flight 93 who thwarted the terrorists plan by taking action and taking over. All these lives lost. How could we not be affected?

It seems that every one of us is thinking about our own mortality. That may sound a bit morbid to you, but it really isn't. If you keep it in perspective and realize it is an inevitable part of life it can actually do more help than harm. It frees us up to tell people we love them and to do things we have always wanted to do. Evie and Erin both notice a change since the addition of children to their lives. Without sounding like a bunch of egomaniacs we all realize how our children would suffer at the loss of one or both parents. That is a terrifying thought to most of us. Elena, DeniseB, Susan and Ellen all mention that they now have a greater appreciation for life and what they have, and a need to let friends and family know how much they are loved. There was a young lady speaking at the services downtown today whose stepfather died in the WTC. She said she had not recently told him how much she loved him and that she would give anything to go back to the morning of 9/11 just to utter the words "I love you" to him. If we walk away with anything from these tragedies it should be that. Tell people you love them. They can be taken from us forever without a moments notice. Tell people you love them. Tell them again.

In rather unique circumstances are BethL and Sophie. Both are career military women serving in Armed Forces. Both women must deal with the daily possibility of being sent to a hostile country at any moment. They both agree that 9/11 gave them a deeper appreciation of life.

As far as a favorite response (this is getting harder and harder to choose) I guess I will choose DeniseW's. It speaks for itself. When asked ***"Do you think about your own mortality? Has this changed since 9/11"?*** DeniseW responded: "9/11 definitely changed me. I was in the city when it happened. Alan was at Newark Airport waiting for his flight to Japan. When the planes hit, all phone communication was stopped. I could not get in touch with anyone. I couldn't reach Alan to see if he was ok, or my ex-husband to check on my daughter. Then the city closed down and mass hysteria broke out. I could not get off Manhattan Island. There were F16s flying above us and soot covered everything and everyone. People were just walking up from downtown. I will never forget this day. I truly believed it was the end of the world, and in a way it was. When I finally got home I hugged my daughter, mother and husband so tightly I think I hurt them. I will always remember this day and the days that followed. I will never forget how fragile and fleeting life is".

Here are the rest of our thoughts:

Judy: "How can you not think about your own mortality? It's going to happen. I try very hard to stay healthy. I eat right, exercise, drink 64 oz of water, take calcium supplements, have all my check ups. I think 9/11 changed everyone. I really feel like I lost my innocence that day. It scared me to death. I went and got both my children out of school, I needed to have them with me. I suddenly became afraid of the most ordinary things like bridges, planes and even our mail. We are the Trenton post office and had to deal with Anthrax. For the first time in my life I did not feel safe. Coming from Long Island and having spent several years working in and around the WTC, I felt personally attacked. I literally ache for the poor families of all the victims. I cannot imagine their pain. I organized a candle lighting in our neighborhood the Saturday after the attacks and we had over 100 neighbors and friends come. We formed a circle, lit candles and sang patriotic songs. It was so sad, but so beautiful too".

Evie: "I have thought about it more than ever since my daughter, Cecelia, was born, and now even more since 9/11. The saying "life is too short" seems so much truer now. 9/11 filled me with such deep sorrow and pain for the families of the victims. At the same time, it also made me so much more appreciative of what I have. It made me angry about the relationship that my husband and I threw away—we had a choice, these people had no choice when they lost their loved ones. All in all, it made me more aware of living in the moment—it is all we are guaranteed".

Sophie: "My mortality is something I am aware of because due to my position in the military, I can get sent to a dangerous area and be in harms way. Since 9/11 I feel that I have made my peace with God and that God will accept me into heaven when my time comes. I must say that January 2001 had a greater impact on me than 9/11. I was focused on biblical prophecies and how the turn of the century might play itself out. I talked to some people I consider "subject matter experts" and came to peace with it".

Ellen: "Yes, I think about it more now than before 9/11. I am still not as afraid as some people are about flying or terrorism. Don't get me wrong; I believe that terrorism is evil and cowardly. I have always been a firm believer that "when it's your time, it's your time". Therefore, it is important to continue to live your life to the fullest and to try and do that with my husband and children, family and friends everyday. If anything, 9/11 has given me a new respect for the words courage, human love and compassion and I have a deeper sense of appreciation for all that I have and am able to give".

Erin: "I am afraid of dying for my children's sake. I know what a hole this will leave in their lives. I don't think 9/11 changed me. I think it just reaffirms what I believe. I think people act badly to one another because something is missing from their lives. They make themselves feel better by making others feel worse. How sad that the only way you can elevate yourself is by tearing others down. If we all had a true sense of self worth, we could see the worthiness in others".

BethL: "When my number is up, it's up. I have had a few "not too close" calls. I will either die a fantastic death or peacefully leave this world in my sleep. No sense fretting over something of which I have no control. I lost friends in 9/11 and have friends who lost many family and friends. I realize that you have to make every moment count. As a Medical Service Officer in the US Army, my life will never be the same. I spend most of my days working on issues dealing with Operation Enduring Freedom. I now know what it feels like to put someone else in harms way. My job is to make sure that they are as prepared as possible before leaving South West Asia (SWA). I am more compassionate about others and more passionate about life".

DeniseB: "Yes, I think about my own mortality. I think 9/11 has made us all appreciate our families more and the little things in life".

Tracy: "Yes, I think about my mortality. 9/11 changed me a lot. I know people who did not survive the WTC collapse. You just can't take life for granted. You have to let the people that matter to you know how you feel. I don't know if having worked in downtown Manhattan made it worse, but I have that 'it could have been me' feeling. I still cry when I think about that day".

Jenny: "I guess I have always thought about my own mortality. Even as a kid I was never the type who thought I would never die. I almost died when I was 15, so that has always affected the way I thought about things. There are some things you can't control, but there are lots of things you can. I don't know that 9/11 changed that for me, as much as it reinforced it. Losing people, having friends who lost people, knowing people who could have been there but weren't, and thinking of the tragedy, the horror, and the sadness of it, all for nothing. We've all been affected".

Elena: "Yes, I do think of my own mortality now that I have children. I was never afraid to fly in an airplane or try something new until I had kids. This has not changed because of 9/11. I really believe in a case like this that if I am meant to be where something devastating is going to happen, and then I will be there. What has changed is that it is a reminder of how sudden death can be and that I need to make sure everyday that my husband and family know how much I love them".

Priscilla: "I can't say that I think of my mortality often, and no I don't think 9/11 changed that. I am a big believer in 'if it's your time, it's your time'. God has a big plan for us all".

BethR: "I occasionally think about my own mortality and more so since 9/11. The thing that bothers me most about it is the effect it would have on my children. The loss of a mother at a very young age would be so difficult for them. It's hard enough when you are an adult".

Nancy: "I don't really worry about my own mortality. All I seem to care about is the safety and well being of my family. 9/11 has definitely made me more nervous about flying with my family, but I guess we cannot live in fear. If anything we need to realize that we should live life to the fullest. I even let my husband, Matt, get a motorcycle"!

Susan: "I don't really think about my own mortality in the sense that someday I am going to die, but since 9/11 I do realize that everyday is truly a gift. Life can be forever altered in a minute. We all learned that from 9/11. You have to make the most out of it as you go along. Petty arguments are a waste of time. You need to let the people you love know that you love them. You should enjoy the time you are together. There is an email that has gone around so many times since 9/11 'if I knew I would not be here tomorrow I would have...' So, say the things you want to say, do the things you want to do, don't waste your time on stupid, insignificant stuff".

DeniseW: "9/11 definitely changed me. I was in the city when it happened. Alan was at Newark Airport waiting for his flight to

Japan. When the planes hit all phone communication was stopped. I could not get in touch with anyone. I couldn't reach Alan to see if he was ok, or my ex-husband to check on my daughter. Then the city closed down and mass hysteria broke out. I could not get off Manhattan Island. There were F16s flying above us and soot covered everything and everyone. People were just walking up from downtown. I will never forget this day. I truly believed it was the end of the world, and in a way it was. When I finally got home I hugged my daughter, mother and husband so tightly I think I hurt them. I will always remember this day and the days that followed. I will never forget how fragile and fleeting life is".

CHAPTER 24—"ARE YOU A GOOD PERSON? A GOOD WIFE, MOTHER, DAUGHTER, EMPLOYEE, FRIEND?

I think this is a question that probably plagues most people at some time in their life. I often wonder, at the moment, when I am feeling proud of myself for being a good mother, have I sacrificed being a good wife, or worse yet, vice versa? I think most women try to be good at everything. Everyone interviewed here is a product of the sexual revolution. We were born in the radical 60's, were teens in the drug obsessed 70s and young adults in the 'me generation' of the 80's (one of my favorite decades). We were brought up to believe that not only could we be a good wife, mother, daughter, friend and employee, but that *should* be very good at all these things. Our generation of women was raised to do it all, to be superwomen, which of course we all are. If you don't believe me just peruse the responses given here. Every one of us is fairly confident that we rate at least a 'good' in all or most of the above mentioned categories. As BethR stated sometimes we must sacrifice one category in order to be 'good' at another. BethR notes that she feels confident that she is a good Mom, but may need to spend more time on her 'least squeaky wheel', her husband Joe. At this point in our lives many of us have young children. For better or worse they require our full, undivided attention and affection and we, as their mothers, give it freely and without reservation. We all feel that we are good Mothers and this is an amazing feat! I constantly refer to parenthood as "the toughest job you will ever love". A single day of parenting will tire you out more than running the New York marathon. It is exhausting mentally and physically. And yet somehow we are finding the strength to be more than just a good Mom (like that isn't enough?). Tracy, Evie and Elena all feel that they are good daughters. Erin says that Frank thinks she is a good wife (at least most of the time). I think that is a tremendous compliment. Most men think we can't do enough for them. I think I just started to like Frank even more! BethL and Sophie feel they are good and hard working employees, a credit to our men and ladies in uniform. But above all else, we all feel that we are good people. Now we are not being a conceited bunch of over confident women. We are basing this on how we treat others, our capacity to love and have sympathy for those less fortunate than ourselves (remember we are an incredibly 'lucky' and 'blessed' group) and even by what people tell us. Many of us also mention that sometimes we are not so good. We all need a little work. Perhaps we could call our parents more, or not take them for granted as Evie says. We might try being a little more patient with our children and not yell so easily. I know I personally could use a little work on this one. How about cutting our husbands some slack? BethR and Ellen might agree to this one. So are we a perfect bunch of Stepford wives, mothers, daughters etc...absolutely not. Who in their right mind would want to be that perfect? We can continue to trudge along working everyday at being the best that we can be.

I think everyone's answers were good, though I do have a favorite. When asked the question *"Are you a good person? A Good wife, mother, daughter, employee, friend etc."?* Erin's response was this: "One of the most meaningful things my mother said to me while I was visiting with her one day, was what a good person I was. Frank thinks that I am a good wife, at least most of the time. My boys have said that I am the best Mommy in the whole world (but then again they have said some things not quite so nice, so, hmmm…let's think about that one). I try, that's all I can say".

I think Erin has gotten verification from 3 very credible sources, her mother, her husband and her children. Obviously Erin is doing something right here. What a great compliment in life to have the people most important to you feel that you are the great at what you do (being a daughter, mom and wife) and they are not afraid to tell her—equally as important. Personally, and I am going out on a limb here, I think Erin deserves a little raise, what do you think?

The rest of us had this to say:

Judy: "This was a tough one for me and I had to come back to it a few times. I think basically, yes, I am a good person, a good wife, mother, daughter and friend. I think sometimes I am better at one and need some work on another and then the next week it flip-flops. I constantly work at it all".

Evie: "I'd like to think so. I do try to be good, but there are some days that I know I could be a lot better. I am a good daughter, but I know there are times when I feel that I take my parents for granted. Good wife? I guess not. Good mother? I think so. I work at it and it's hard work. There are times when my patience is thin and I need to work on not just reacting to a situation, but handling it and getting through it. There is no one giving me raises and promotions at this job, but if my daughter's happiness is a barometer, then I guess I am doing well".

Sophie: "Overall I would say that I am a good Christian, mother, wife, employee, sister and daughter, in that order. I make mistakes and sometimes I get just plain lazy. I own up to these things and just 'keep on truckin'".

Ellen: "So everyone tells me! I am a great daughter. So I think. I am a good wife, however, I think being a wife takes years of practice. Sometimes it's hard to remember that I have a partner who wants to be my 'better half'. I so want to control our lives and forget that Bob has some say in this too. So for that reason I am not a *great* wife. Yes, I am a good mother. I love, love, love, being a mother. My children have give me the greatest satisfaction in my life thus far".

Erin: "One of the most meaningful things my mother said to me, while I was visiting with her one day, was what a good person I was. Frank thinks that I am a good wife, at least most of the time. My boys have said that I am the best Mommy in the whole world (but then again they have said some things not quite so nice, so, hmmm…let's think about that one). I try, that's all I can say".

DeniseB: "I believe that I am a good person. I don't think people have said negative things about me".

BethL: "I always try to consider others when making decisions. I try not to be selfish and to be generous to those who have not been as blessed as I have been. I should call my folks more often and tell them how much I love, miss and cherish them. I have decided to dedicate my life to my marriage and so has my husband. We're good to each other and good for each other. I don't know what kind of mom I will be. I am a dedicated, hard working and honest. I don't work by the hour but by the finished product. I care about the soldiers under my command and those in their care".

Tracy: "Yes to all of the above, but a lousy housekeeper"!

Jenny: "I think I am a good person, although I'm never quite as good as I could be".

Elena: "I like to think I am a good person. It is one very important thing to me to try and work hard to be a good person and give my all at everything I do. There are times when I see myself not being such a good wife, mother, daughter etc. and I try and change that".

Priscilla: "Yes to all of them! I probably put my job in last place and it therefore may not get the 'best of me'. I tend to work *smart* not necessarily *hard* if that makes any sense".

BethR: "I think that I am a good person. I also think that I am an excellent daughter and employee. I hope that I am a good Mom; sometimes I wish I had more patience, but I really do try to be good at it. Wife, well you would have to ask Joe about that one. Of all the choices I would probably have to say that I am worst at being a wife. I don't know why, but since my husband is not a child he falls to the end of my 'to do' list. I should make more time for him, but he is the least 'squeaky wheel' in my house".

Nancy: "I try to be a good person to everyone in my life. I can never say 'no' to anyone, except for maybe my poor husband".

Susan: "I think that I am a good person. I am not yet a wife or mother, but if I was I think I would be good at that too. I am a good employee, my parents taught me responsibility so I take my job seriously, and I work hard and try to do over and above what is expected of me. I am a kind and caring person and I am a good friend, daughter, sister and aunt".

DeniseW: "Yes, yes, yes and yes".

CHAPTER 25—WHAT PERSONAL EVENT OR EVENTS IN YOUR LIFE HAVE REALLY CHANGED OR SHAPED YOU?

In reality the events that have shaped the women we are today are too numerous and sometimes seemingly insignificant to list. Almost everything we do or don't do has shaped our lives in some way, it's just a matter of whether we realize it or not. Take, for instance, your 4th grade teacher who made it fun to come to school and learn everyday. Could she be the reason you became a teacher yourself? The seed may have been planted many, many years before you ever made a conscious decision to teach. What about your decision on which college to attend? Could the fact that the college you finally chose just had that cozy feeling have been as much a factor as what it offered academically? Think of all the changes that would have taken place in your life if you simply choose a different college; different friends, different major, different job opportunities, different place to live, and for some people like Erin, a different spouse—now we could go on and on from here. It is as Jenny alludes, a compilation of all our life experiences that shape us, yet sometimes there is an event or experience that is so profound it seems to define the essence of who we really are, or better yet, who we have become. For several of us that event was the birth of our children. There are as many reasons for this as there are children and at last count there are at least 30 children represented here. For me, the birth of my children was a truly enlightening and faith affirming event that literally changed my attitude about life. For Evie, Ellen and Priscilla having children brought them a love so deep and all encompassing it was unlike anything that they had ever experienced before. It is almost a given that we would mention having children as an event, or events as the case may be, that has changed us. For the first time in our lives we were actually responsible for the safety, care and upbringing of someone other than ourselves. Talk about waking up and smelling the coffee. Children tend to put your priorities right the hell in order. They come first, you come last. Yet, obviously, there is more to us than our children. We lived entire lives before they came to be with us. Sometimes something painful in our past can leave an everlasting impression on us, no matter how hard we struggle to move on. For Ellen the very emotional relationship and subsequent break up with a college boyfriend left self-esteem issues that have taken her years to overcome. For Sophie a much more complex issue of abuse led to a life-long desire to control her environment. For DeniseB the invaluable experience of living overseas in Japan and London have changed her sense of self. It seems like many of us have learned valuable though painful lessons from our life-shaping events. I guess this is really the whole idea isn't it? So often people tell us a situation is what you choose to make of it. If life gives you lemons, make lemonade. The important thing is what you do with it. I personally don't know if I would have had the strength that Sophie must have had as a child. I don't know many people who would have been able to pull themselves together so well and so completely after being a victim of sexual abuse. Certainly a life-changing event isn't it.

If we really think about it, it is not only these huge events that shape us, these almost historic things that happen in our lives. It is as much the little everyday things, as Jenny mentions, that happen over and over, going to work and meeting new people that tend to shape or change us as well.

Here we go with the best response again. Best, favorite, whatever. I never though this part would be so hard. I think I am going to have to go with Priscilla. When asked the question, ***"What personal event or events in your life have really changed or shaped you"?*** Priscilla wrote: "As I said in one of the earlier questions, the death of my father at a relatively young age, he was only 58. This had such a profound impact on my outlook and idea of what really matters to me. I try not to sweat the small stuff, so in some ways my father's death has helped me become a more focused person. Becoming a parent has been, thus far, the most incredibly rewarding and fulfilling experience yet. It is the best! Until you experience it, it is hard to believe how much you can love someone, it's a much deeper love than you even feel toward your spouse, mother, siblings etc…it is just in a class by itself and can't be compared to any other kind of love".

I just liked the fact that Priscilla took the very sad death of her father and reworked it so that she walked away with a very positive lesson, life is short and we should concentrate on the truly important things. Some people go through their entire lives without ever really finding this out. Priscilla, on the other hand, learned this in her early 20's.

Here's what the rest of us feel has either shaped or changed us:

Judy: "I think that 2 related events help shape who I am today, fertility problems and the birth of my son, Tommy. If you are undergoing fertility treatments you must make a 200% commitment to the process and make it the top priority in your life or it will not work. People who have never had fertility problems have no idea the constant pain and anguish involved. There is total devastation every month when your period arrives. I had horrible, mean things said to me by people who were supposed to love me, and this unnerved me. Infertility takes the fun out of sex, diminishing it to a timed chore. I think it taught me to be a more compassionate person. I learned just how much I wanted to have a baby and what I was willing to go through to get one (anything and everything). I learned which of my friends would always be there for me when I needed a shoulder to cry on. I learned that I wanted to stay home with my baby. When Tommy finally arrived I felt like the luckiest, most blessed person in the world. I still do".

Evie: "Being born in the middle of 5 children has made me a more easy-going, middle of the road, peace-maker type person. Going away to college at Siena made me learn that I can do for myself. It made me appreciate my parents, but also to know that I can rely on myself to do the responsible thing without being told. I met some of my very best friends there too! Being a Mom has really changed me. It has made me realize what is really important. Now I know a love deeper than I ever could have imagined before. Going through a separation after being with someone for 16 years has been traumatic. Adding on betrayal and infidelity was just devastating. But with the help of family, friends and a good counselor, I can actually say that I am coming out a better, more self-confident person than ever before. And believe me, I never thought I would ever say those words".

Sophie: "I am the oldest daughter in my family. I had a lot or responsibility thrust upon me when my Dad retired and went back to school when I was 11. My mom went back to work and I was in charge of my younger siblings after school. My brother was a year older, but very irresponsible. That and being a survivor of sexual abuse has mostly fed my need to be in control or in charge. I am very protective of those around me".

Ellen: "Most assuredly the birth of my children. Giving life to another human being has to be the most significant life-altering event of my life. And to do it three times, each one was new and different experience. Prior to those moments, a devastating break up with my college boyfriend had a profound effect on how, to this day, I view people's honesty and integrity, especially men.

To have loved someone so completely and have been so naïve to his or her true self still haunts me for some strange reason. It was the foundation for some of my worst insecurities and it has taken me close to 15 years to really feel more secure with myself. I cannot believe that even though I was so young that I allowed myself to base my whole sense of self-worth on another individual's opinion. When I met Bob, I instantly knew that this man was different. That in itself was a very significant event that changed my life forever".

Erin: "My marriage and the birth of my children. They have both defined my life".

DeniseB: "The death of my parents has left a void. I am sometimes jealous of other people my age who still have one or both of their parents alive. It was hard to lose my father, but losing my mother was something different entirely. I had always dreamed, like every little girl, that my father would walk me down the aisle, but that can't happen now, though I still hope to marry someday. On a happier note, living overseas taught me to be self-reliant. It made me realize that I can do things on my own and nothing bad will happen to me. Yes, some people do look at you differently when you are alone, but I have seen parts of the world that most people will never see (I lived in Japan and London) and have made lasting friendships from my travels".

BethL: "Visiting other countries made me realize how truly lucky we are to be Americans. Even the poorest people here are much better off than the average person in some other countries. Being married has changed me too. I no longer need to look for my best friend, he's right here with me. 9/11/01—I am not going to live in fear".

Tracy: "Having children".

Jenny: "I think what has really shaped me are a million little events and non-events over the course of my life. But if I had to think about external things that shaped me, I would think of major historical events that have occurred in my life, like 9/11. Personal experiences like meeting people who have become my dearest friends, going to college, working and traveling have also contributed to who I am today".

Elena: "Most definitely having children"

Priscilla: "As I said in one of the earlier questions, the death of my father at a relatively young age, he was only 58. This had such a profound impact on my outlook and idea of what really matters to me. I try not to sweat the small stuff, so in some ways my father's death has helped me become a more focused person. Becoming a parent has been, thus far, the most incredibly rewarding and fulfilling experience yet. It is the best! Until you experience it, it is hard to believe how much you can love someone, it's a much deeper love than you even feel toward your spouse, mother, siblings etc…it is just in a class by itself and can't be compared to any other kind of love".

BethR: "I still think the event that has shaped me most was becoming a mother and I kind of covered that in a previous question".

Nancy: "Moving to New York City was definitely a life-changing event for me. It really opened me up to a different world that I had not been previously exposed to as a girl from the mid-west. I think I am more open-minded and worldlier now because of that move I made in my 20's. I try to impose that understanding and openness to my boys".

Susan: "I think everything we do and the choices we constantly make continually change and shape us. I made the greatest friends I have here in Albany, if I had chosen a college other than Siena, this would all be different. Right before my father died I got laid off from IBM and these were two difficult things for me to be dealing with and both of them changed me. I couldn't replace my father and I missed him and always will. I'm sure I could have used his help many times over the years. Leaving IBM changed me too. I have a new career in new city with new friends. Of course there is 9/11 too, that day changed everyone's life. It made me realize what is important, like family and friends and spending time with them. I live far away from most of my family but now I go home more often. I think it is important for me to spend time with Annie and Chris who lost their father, Chris on 9/11".

DeniseW: "My divorce and subsequent custody battle with my ex-husband. I have become more bitter and less trusting because of this".

CHAPTER 26—WHAT HAS CHANGED MOST ABOUT YOU FROM 30 TO 40? HAS THIS CHANGE BEEN POSTIVE OR NEGATIVE?

Well, it is obviously the fact that our boobs are now several inches lower than they used to be! This is true whether or not you have had children, but actually no one mentioned that. It seems, from reading these responses, that quite possibly the biggest changes in our lives may occur in puberty and our 30's. In puberty our bodies go through the requisite changes, we get our breasts, pubic and underarm hair, hips and of course our *friend*, the much dreaded period. Personally, I never understood the *friend* metaphor, not one of my friends has even been as much trouble as my period. Anyway, back to the topic. We go through mood swings during puberty and our sense of self and body image changes, usually for the worse, but thank God, temporarily. Well guess what? All this happens again in our 30's, mostly toward the end. Our periods become longer, heavier and less reliable. We can no longer be sure of just when it will arrive. Our mood swings, mostly due to PMS, are more intense, and last longer. Our boobs sag, our hips are probably bigger and we are even getting zits again! How unfair is this? But perhaps the biggest change is not a physical one, but a mental one. Adjectives like 'comfortable' keep cropping up in the responses in reference to our moods, our selves, our opinions, and our work. Many of us feel that we are now more assertive; we speak up and share our opinion like never before. Have you ever been in these situations? You are returning an item to a local store, the sales clerk is being less than helpful and bordering on rude—do we take it? NO!! We ask for the Manager! Your food is served to you cold, do you eat it? NO, back it goes! You have sat waiting in your Doctor's office (with 1 or more screaming children) for over 20 minutes? Do we sit quietly? NO!! We complain! I remember as a child being so embarrassed when my mother did this, and now, well let's just say my boys are going to spend the vast majority of their youth being embarrassed. The thing is we are not making trouble or being mean. We are entitled to politeness by our sales clerk (as long as we are not being rude to them), hot food and for our Doctors to run at least close to on time (emergencies always arise and we should be patient in these instances). It's just that in our 20's we would NEVER have spoken up. We would sit there and just take it. So now here we are at 40 being assertive, outspoken, women in control. Look out world. What is even better is that several of the girls mentioned that their self-esteem has finally taken its place in the foreground. Many of the girls have overcome years of insecurities and finally feel that they have arrived at 40 confident and self-assured. Ellen, BethL and Tracy all mention this as one the things that have changed most about them in the past 10 or so years. They mention that this is a positive change and I totally agree. Jenny and Erin mention the loss of their waistline. I am not sure if that was supposed to be funny. I see them both at least once a year, in a bathing suit no less, and I have to tell you, they look pretty much the same as they did in college. I certainly don't notice a change in their waistlines (bitches). Evie notices a change in her priorities and I have to say that I now see the glass as "half full" rather than "half empty". Both of us feel these have been positive changes for us. So maybe instead of calling this mid-life, we might want to call it "puberty revisited".

Not all of us feel that we have really changed all that much. Susan and Jenny both feel that they are fundamentally the same people, with a few minor adjustments here and there.

Once again I really did like all the answers, but BethL stands out for me. When asked*, "What has changed most about you from 30—40? Has this change been positive or negative"?* BethL responded: "I am more assertive. I have always been smart, I just am able to share it more now. I am more tolerant of others and their beliefs. I realize more than ever that I must appreciate everyone and everything in my life. I had some low points, but for the most part I feel better about myself now than I did 10 years ago".

I think her response just speaks volumes about what turning 40 is all about. The rest of us had some pretty interesting things to say too:

Judy: "Another one I had to come back to but here it is. I have gone from expecting the worst outcome of a situation to just praying for the strength to deal with whatever comes my way. I have changed completely from a pessimist to an optimist. A few years ago my Mom found out she had to have open-heart surgery again. In my early 30s this would have terrified me because I would just anticipate the worst. But I knew, I can't even begin to explain it, but I just knew that she was going to be all right. And she was. That's how I deal with all the little things that bog me down now. I can do arthritis, I can do hypothyroidism, I can do gall bladder trouble and I can do just about anything else life throws my way (just keep my kids healthy!). In my early 30s I would have wondered why God was punishing me with these things, now I know that God gives me strength to handle them as best I can. I think this has been an overwhelmingly positive change in my life and made me a better wife and mother".

Evie: "I would have to say my priorities. I wasn't a mother at 30. Some of the things that were important to me then, seem ridiculous to me now. I don't think I am as selfish as I was then. I would say this has been a positive change".

Sophie: "From 30 to 40 I have become more comfortable with myself and my moods. I have definite opinions about things that I feel free to share when asked. If my reason for my opinion is 'just because I think so' that is ok too. Yet I am more affected by disappointments in my ability to complete goals that I have set for myself, and I worry that I may get lazy and set more attainable goals and not challenge myself enough".

Ellen: "My ability to cope with a stressful situation seems to be less than it was. I definitely think this is a negative change. As insecure as I felt about myself in my 20s and 30's stress seemed to be less of a factor. I do have a much stronger sense of self now. I think I am a much better judge of character and I have realized more of my goals. I still have a zany 'we can do and we should do' side to me. That has changed much over the years. I laugh more now that I have children. Not always out loud, but I laugh. I have no desire to work as I did in my 20's and early 30's (my husband does not know this yet). I love being home. Although I am cranky about all that I have to do sometimes. Overall I feel better about me, and that is positive".

Erin: "My waistline and that is a negative change".

DeniseB: "I think I am more comfortable about myself and where I am in my life".

BethL: "I am more assertive. I have always been smart, I just am able to share it more now. I am more tolerant of others and their beliefs. I realize more than ever that I must appreciate everyone and everything in my life. I had some low points, but for the most part I feel better about myself now than I did 10 years ago".

Tracy: "I am comfortable with who I am now. I also feel that it is just fine if some people don't like me. These are both changes for the better".

Jenny:"My waistline! Really, I think I am very much the same as I was eight or so years ago. I have a different profession, but I see that as an extension of who I am. I've been a public servant for the past

14 years, first in state government, then county and now as a teacher. I've just narrowed my focus to concentrate more on the individual. I think this has been for the better. I have changed where I live, which is a little of both. I love being near my family, but I miss my friends. I think those changes helped me to embrace and grow a little more. I have always been the type who didn't do well with change. But change can be good".

Elena: "During this 10 year span my children entered elementary school. It has been a huge change for me. I have so many new friends because they are the families of my children's friends. I have more social activities with different groups of people. My weekends have changed due to the kid's activities. Because of their ages I have become very active in their school and started working as a substitute teacher. These have all been positive changes for me".

Priscilla: "I only worked part-time at 30-years old, so I am busier now. Sometimes the business is good and constructive and sometimes I feel like I am not caught up with anything".

BethR: "Aside from getting better looking? I think I have become more community minded and less focused on me. Some of that is related to having kids and the type of involvements that can naturally flow from that like, twins clubs, PTA, girl scouts, boy scouts etc. And now I am an official member of the Kings Park Fire department. What next? I have some ideas, but they involve the kind of commitment that would require my children to be a little more self-sufficient".

Nancy: "The thing that has changed most is now I have a sense of purpose. I used to sit around and wait for things to happen to me, now I go after what I want".

Susan: "This is a tough question. I don't know that I have changed much in the last ten years. I think I am pretty much the same person I was ten or so years ago. I guess maybe some of the things I like to do are different. I much prefer going out to a nice dinner with friends or to someone's house for dinner than going to a bar. Actually I don't like going anyplace that is crowded. I no longer find it fun to be pushed and shoved all night. I no longer feel the need to go out every weekend, sometimes it is nice to just stay home and relax. I get enough of the bar scene at work. Besides, I don't bounce back the way I used to!"

DeniseW: "I am much more responsible than I used to be. At 30 I still considered myself a kid, at 40 I can no longer keep that vision. I am more realistic, but I still love to dream".

CHAPTER 27—ARE THERE CERTAIN THINGS YOU FEEL YOU CAN'T WEAR BECAUSE OF YOUR AGE? HAS YOUR SENSE OF STYLE CHANGED?

I don't know about you, but I constantly look at things in magazines, or what some movie star is wearing and I think one of two things. First one; "that might work at the MTV Music Awards, but no place else", and second "She is too old to be wearing that outfit". Doesn't anyone tell these people what they look like? I guess most, maybe even all of us here are a bit conservative when it comes to our appearance. Remember, we grew up when the "preppy" look was all the rage (I pray on a regular basis that the preppy look will make a comeback so my boys will look like *nice boys* and not baggy pants hoodlums). Many women subscribe to the notions that if it looks good, wear it. Please define *"looks good"?* Just because something fits you or because you are in good shape does not mean it looks good on you. Susan uses the example of spandex, saying that no one really belongs in or looks good in spandex. Maybe looks good should go hand in hand with the word, oh and this is one of my favorite words, *appropriate*. I hate inappropriateness. I think if you are going to a semi-formal cocktail party you should be in a nice dress or pant suit. If you show up in jeans and a T-shirt, this is inappropriate. Conversely if you are going to your child's soccer game you don't need to be in spiked heels, braless, in a tank top with shorts that are too tight and riding up your ass (first of all doesn't that hurt?). Again, *inappropriate*. We used to have more rules that governed fashion, such as never wear white or black to a wedding, no white shoes, shorts, skirt, pants or bags, before Memorial Day or after Labor Day. I know a few people who still subscribe to these, but not many. Just about everyone has worn black to a wedding, most of us are New Yorkers and we live in black, we wear it everywhere. Maybe I am too much of a stickler for inappropriateness but I think there are few things more pathetic then 45-year-old women wearing styles clearly meant for their teenage daughters. Susan and I clearly agree on this. I wont go into detail or name names, but we have all seen these women in People magazine. There are certainly enough different styles out there that today's more mature woman can still look young and sexy without looking like she rifled through the closet of her 12 year old daughter!

I think several of the women make some other good points, BethL and Ellen both feel that fashion has more to do with body type than age. This is certainly a valid point. We have all seen women (like the one mentioned above at the soccer game) that wear their clothes way too tight, or just in an unflattering manner. By age 40 most people should have a pretty good sense of what looks good on them in terms of color and style. None of this involves an eye for fashion or buying expensive designer clothes, all it really involves is being honest with yourself and occasionally asking the opinion of someone you trust. Ultimately you should go with what is comfortable for you and your lifestyle, and with what looks good on you. Erin, Tracy, Jenny and Elena are all in agreement here. Sophie noted that recently she has changed her style a bit, she doesn't mention if she made this change because of her age, or because of her body image, but never the less she has made a change.

So maybe everyone isn't as obsessed with, here we go with that word again, *inappropriateness,* as I am, maybe it was the way I was raised.

In our house you dressed up for the holidays. My mother wore a skirt or nice slacks (do we even use that word anymore?) to go over to my aunt's house six blocks away. She had her evening bag, and perfume for everyday and one for special occasions (Chanel #5) and so I guess, the seeds were sown in me! Thanks Mom.

Favorite response? I am going to choose Nancy's. When asked, *"Are there certain things you feel you can't wear because of your age? Has your sense of style changed"?* She replied: "It's funny, but I have been getting more daring in my old age. I think it may be because I have started to lose weight and have the desire to look good again. So I am actually wearing tighter fitting clothes and sleeveless shirts again. I refuse to succumb to looking like a middle-aged housewife. Watch out you young 'uns".

I like Nancy's answer because she is feeling more comfortable with her body and showing off what looks good. She remains stylish and fun without sacrificing her dignity.

Here is how we all feel about fashion:

Judy: "Yes, I feel too old to wear that whole peasant look that is popular now, although I really didn't care for it the first time around in the 70s, so I don't really feel like I am missing anything. My sense of style has absolutely improved. I find that I prefer to be in a little dress or skirt instead of shorts in the summer because it is a cleaner, neater look and it makes me feel more grown up. I try to stay current with today's fashion without going trendy. I love my 'stuff' as one of my friends says (meaning my Kate Spade bags, Burberry, Chanel, etc…)".

Evie: "Well, I can't shop in the junior department or in stores like The Limited, but I was never much for the real 'fad' styles anyway. I don't think my style has changed too much. For me, it has as much to do with my weight as it does with my age. I do try to keep up without looking foolish".

Sophie: "In the last year I have noticed that my clothing style has changed greatly. A year ago I was still wearing belly shirts and jeans. I am still quite casual but I now own more suits and I feel more reserved when I wear them".

Ellen: "Not because I am 40, but because my body won't allow it! I personally would not want to offend anyone. I choose not to look matronly. I have always prided myself on looking put together and that has not changed. ".

Erin: "No, I wear what I think looks good. I've never been much into name brands or trends. If I like it, I wear it".

DeniseB: "No, my style hasn't changed much at all. I am still somewhat preppy".

BethL: "Fashion shouldn't be about age, but about body type. There are things that I wouldn't wear when I was twenty because I have large breasts. Well, that hasn't changed. Some people really need to put a full-length mirror in their homes or get an honest best friend. Friends shouldn't let friends dress poorly. I was very preppy in high school and became a bit funkier in college. I enjoy wearing clothes that are tasteful yet fun. I love bright colors and patterned materials (it hides flaws!)".

Tracy: "Yes, there are things I wont wear because of my age. I like to dress in a comfortable, casual, neat look. I try to look put together when leaving the house, but some days I just can't be bothered. I feel better when I dress better".

Jenny: "No, anything I look good in I will wear. I've never been trendy so it that is not an issue. You're always allowed to wear jeans and tie dye shirts, it's just the places you can wear them to that keep changing. Do I wear bikinis now? No, the last time a bikini graced this body I was 13. I have a thing about my stomach. I don't show it to people. I don't know why, maybe it is that Catholic good girl thing again".

Elena: "My sense of style has not changed much because I have always been a T-shirt and jeans kind of girl. There are outfits that I cannot wear because of my age. I would look ridiculous in those trendy hippie outfits and clunky shoes. Besides the fact that I think I would look ridiculous because of my age, I also no longer have the figure for it".

Priscilla: "Sure I would never wear a skimpy spaghetti strap tank top (too revealing), but I probably would not have worn it 10 years ago either. I am a pretty conservative dresser hailing from conservative Connecticut and that hasn't changed".

BethR: "Well I am not about to get a belly ring, even though it wouldn't cause me any pain since I no longer have any feeling around my belly button due to my pregnancy with the twins. A bikini would be out for similar reasons. None of that is related to the 'age' issue so much as what age has done to my body. My sense of style has changed too, but I think it is more related to what is 'in style' and what looks good on me more than my age".

Nancy: "It's funny, but I have been getting more daring in my old age. I think it may be because I have started to lose weight and have the desire to look good again. So I am actually wearing tighter fitting clothes and sleeveless shirts again. I refuse to succumb to looking like a middle-aged housewife. Watch out you young 'uns".

Susan: "Yes I do. I don't think a 40-year old should dress like a teenager. I mean we can still wear jeans and sweats and t-shirts, but I don't think *anyone* should be walking around in spandex, not even a teenager. Just because we are turning 40 doesn't mean that we have to dress like our grandmother's did in a polyester housedress. There are plenty of nice, fashionable clothes for us out there. I don't know if my sense of style has changed. I have always liked to dress casually and comfortably. I like a pair of jeans or khakis and a sweater. I just bought a whole bunch of print capris with cute tops for the summer. I think people should worry about wearing appropriate clothes for their body type as opposed to their age".

DeniseW: "Yes, I can't wear belly shirts and those low rise jeans. While I am a size 6 and have a fairly good body, I am very aware that I am no longer a young person. I still try and dress kind of funky, but am finding that increasingly difficult in the misses section, so I usually wind up back in the junior department and just try and be very selective."

CHAPTER 28—DO YOU EVER MISS BEING YOUNGER? WHAT AGE, IF ANY WOULD YOU CHOOSE TO GO BACK TO?

I must admit that I was surprised by the responses to this question. I didn't think so many people missed being younger. The previous questions all seem to indicate that we are happy, confident, secure adults. Well, we are, we are just happy, confident, secure adults who miss being younger. Count me out of this group. I don't know why but I always wanted to be older. Maybe this stems from being a December birthday and always feeling like the young one. To this day I refer to myself as almost a whole year older because so many of my friends have birthdays before mine. Even when pressed to choose a younger age to go back to I picked 35. That was only 4 years ago, and truth be told, I just like the number! Don't get me wrong, I loved high school and college and the years that followed, I just don't want to go back. Quite a few of the girls disagree with me (this is good it makes the reading more interesting). Erin, DeniseB, BethL, Tracy, Nancy, DeniseW, BethR and Priscilla all miss being younger. Erin laments not appreciating her youth more. Nancy, BethR and DeniseB all picked the exact same age they would choose to go back to, 25. I'll let you read about their reasons. Tracy would like to go back and revisit high school and college, but she has one condition—that she is able to know then what she knows now. This sounds like a good idea to me, you could avoid all the mistakes you made, study harder, date the right boys, wear better clothes and not sweat the small stuff and this time enjoy it even more. Evie, Ellen, Elena, Susan and Priscilla would all choose to go back to college; Siena should love this because all 5 of them attended college there. I think college is the choice of so many of the girls because it is a time of 'emerging independence' as Ellen so eloquently puts it. It was really the first time for all of us that we were on our own. All our decisions were our own. Good or bad we were the ones deciding whether or not to go to class, what and when we ate, what we spent our money on, how late we stayed out etc. It may have even been the first time we were forced to live with the repercussions of our decisions, for instance failing a test because we spent the night before at Dapper's or The Beer Joint drinking and carousing. Not me personally of course! Never happened.

For those of us who did not particularly miss being younger the reasons were simple. We may feel better about our lives, and ourselves as Sophie does, or as Evie and Elena say, they still feel young. It stands to reason that if you feel young you would not miss being younger. At least that makes sense to me.

OK, well I am not going with my dopey answer as a favorite response here! I am not even sure what I was thinking, or what I was going for when I wrote this!

I do like Jenny's response to this question, so I am going to choose her as my favorite. When asked*: "Do you ever miss being younger? What age, if any would you choose to go back to"?* Jenny responded: "I remember things I did, people I was with and think how much fun it all was. But I am not sure that is the same thing as missing being young or wishing you were still young. To me it was great, but it's still back there in the past. I think it's very sad when people spend too much time focusing on the 'good old days'. It's like Bruce Springsteen's song 'Glory Days'. I remember when I was in high school there was a group of guys who taught there. They had all been members of the state championship basketball team. This is a great accomplishment, don't get me wrong, but they lived in those days, as if it were the high point of their lives and they weren't even 30 yet. They acted like life was all down hill after high school. That's an awful lot of down and not much up. You have to get a life, and to do that you have to learn from your past and appreciate it. My 30's have been great, then again so were my 20's, my teens and my childhood. There's no reason to think the rest of my life won't be just as great. PS I would NEVER be 12 again, not for all the tea in China".

I like what Jenny says about the past having its place in the past. Love it, remember it, cherish it, and just get passed it. I also like that she is looking forward to the future and assuming that it is going to be great.

Here are our little fantasies:

Judy: "I don't miss being younger. Every age, like every person, seemed to have a good and bad side to it. I like the sound of 35. It is so right there in the middle of things. Not too young, yet not too old. If I had to pick I guess, for no good reason really, I would go with 35".

Evie: "I don't think so. I feel better now than I have in a long time, so I am happy where I am. I feel younger, so I don't have the need to *be* younger. Hmmmmm I would like to re-visit my college years just for fun, and just for a visit".

Sophie: "I don't miss being younger. I know so much more now. If I could have my 30 year old body, I could sure go for that"!

Ellen: "I miss being in college. I loved my friends, I loved my boyfriend and I loved my new emerging sense of independence. Nineteen to 23 was pretty great".

Erin: "Sometimes I do miss being younger. I wish I had appreciated my youth more. I might want to try 16-17 for a little while".

DeniseB: "Yes, I miss it sometimes. I might like to go back to being 17 years old and in high school. Yes, that is correct, high school. I would change a couple of things and say yes to a date that may have made my whole prom experience different".

BethL: "YES, especially at 2 in the morning and I am thinking more about my pillow than the beer in my hand. I might choose to go back to the years between 27 and 32".

Tracy: "Yes I do. I would want to go back to high school and college but only if I could know then what I know now".

Jenny: "I remember things I did, people I was with and think how much fun it all was. But I am not sure that is the same thing as missing being young or wishing you were still young. To me it was great, but is still 'back there' I think it's very sad when people spend too much time focusing on the good old days. It's like Bruce's song 'Glory Days'. I remember when I was in high school there was a group of guys who taught there. They had all been members of the state championship basketball team. This is a great accomplishment don't get me wrong. But they lived in those days, as if it were the high point of their lives and they weren't even 30 yet. They acted like life was all down hill after high school. That's an awful lot of down and not much up. You have to get a life, and to do that you have to learn from your past and appreciate it. My 30's have been great, then again so were my 20's, my teens and my childhood. There's no reason to think the rest of my life won't be just as great. PS I would NEVER be 12 again, not for all the tea in China".

Elena: "I don't feel like I have aged all that much even though I know I have. If I were to go back in time I would go back to my college days. I would change some of my behavior and concentrate more on my studies".

Priscilla:"Yes, at times I miss the carefree days of college. I also miss the few years after that when I lived with friends and were all working and having fun, it was like college but we had more responsibility and more money! Not bad. But the rewards of marriage, family and my life today are so great that I never wish I didn't have them".

BethR: "Sometimes I do miss being younger, but it is not something I dwell on, it is more of a passing thought that I get around people who are much younger than me. I would like to go back to around 25 years old. That was a fun time".

Nancy: "I really like my age now because having my kids really made me feel complete. However, being 25 in New York was the absolute best place to be! I was young, carefree and had lots of cash to throw around. Can't beat it".

Susan: "Sometimes I do miss being younger, like about college age. It might be nice to go back to a time where your biggest responsibility was to get to class on time. You didn't have to worry about paying bills and work deadlines. You had all your friends with you everyday to just hang out with. Going to bars, having parties in the dorms, life was a big party and schoolwork (our real reason for being in college) was somehow secondary. I am not really sure I would want to go back and do it all over again though".

DeniseW: "Sometimes, only so that I could relive it again. It felt so carefree. I guess if I had to pick an age to relive it would be 25".

CHAPTER 29—WHAT DO YOU CONSIDER A GOOD DAY? WHAT LITTLE THINGS MAKE YOU HAPPY?

I have only typed in the first four or so responses and I have to say that we are a very sappy group of ladies. I mean my teeth hurt from all the sugar in these responses. Kathie Lee Gifford move over, I have a group of sentimental sweeties, gushing about hugs from our kids and love, love, love and we are about to give you a run for your money. Jenny hit the nail on the head here; she says 'a good day is one where I wake up'. Amen to that. It is definitely at least the *start* of a good day, what happens, and what we do to it from there is pretty much up in the air. I have to say right off the bat that I already know I have two favorite responses. It is not a sappy, drippy one like the rest of us, but it made me laugh. It is DeniseB's. First let me tell you about DeniseB. She is a loving, kind, gentle somewhat quiet person (unless you know her well and know that her nicknames have been Disco and Bubbles). DeniseB rarely complains, is never bitter and generally has a positive attitude. So her answer kind of just blew me away. Here it is. When asked, **"What do you consider a good day? What little things make you happy"?** Our DeniseB responded: "A good day is when no one pisses me off too badly. Not having some idiot cut me off while I'm driving, having someone just be nice to me, getting a phone call or a card from someone I haven't spoken to in a long time (not you Judy that's my fault)". This just cracked me up! I never even hear her talk this way (or hadn't until recently when I was returning home from a long weekend with her and she was driving). Let me tell you, do not cut this girl off! You readers should know by now that I am partial to anything that will make me laugh and that is why I loved this answer so much.

Back to the rest of our 'Kathie Lee' type answers. The Mommy contingent responded much like you would expect us too, and as much as I poke fun at all of us, it is heart warming because it is all true. We all love a hug from our kids, a simple 'I love you mommy' or 'you are the best mommy in the world' is enough to make our entire day a good one. We all love to laugh, either at ourselves, with our kids, or even at our kids! A good day for Evie includes some Yoga, for Sophie it can be completing a project and the sense of satisfaction that brings. For Tracy and Ellen, if they don't have to bitch and moan or yell—at the husband and/or kids, well, that is a *very* good day. I concur by the way. Little things seem to make us happy. Priscilla mentions going to TGIFriday's with friends, Elena feels happy if she is looking good, DeniseB likes to hear from old friends, and I like a good song on the radio. So there you have it. I wish us all good days and all the little things that make us happy.

The envelope please, my second favorite response goes to BethR. When asked, ***"What do you consider a good day? What little things make you happy"?*** her response was this: "A good day is one in which I am busy and productive without being overwhelmed and rushed. It is one in which my children get along and are happy and we even have some time to play. It makes me happy when things go my way, no unexpected stress, maybe having some time to hang out with a friend or even get in an uninterrupted phone call with someone I haven't talked to in a while. And it doesn't hurt if everyone likes what I made for dinner! Or better yet if Joe brings dinner home! See, I am not too tough to please".

This just sounds like a really nice, really simple, really good day.

Read on for some more refreshing, if not syrupy ideas on what a good day is:

Judy: "A good day means many things to me. It is a pain free day. It is a day when the boys ask for kisses and hugs and tell me they miss me for no apparent reason (this always seems to surprise me for some reason). If shopping is included somewhere in that day, even better. It really doesn't take much for me to have a good day; a good song on the radio can make my day and turnaround even my foulest mood. I am happy to report that most of my days are good ones".

Evie: "That is a funny question. A good day is when Cecelia and I wake up happy, manage to keep most of our cereal and milk off the floor; when laughing and singing outweighs crying and whining, when lunch and dinner are finished with a minimum amount of coaxing, and when my little buddy takes a good nap. When I get in a good Yoga class or exercise at home. The best days are when I hear 'I love you Mommy'".

Sophie: "I think any day is a good day when I complete a project either at home or at work and I can put it away. Things that make me happy are singing in church in the choir or during a service. I like seeing friends and smiling, saying 'hello' and hugging. I like to laugh with everyone. My on and off again depression left me unwilling to socialize and laugh for a long time, so now I enjoy it even more".

Ellen: "When I can make it through the day without finding something to gripe to my husband about, and I have finished all of the laundry. The way my children still want to take part in our little evening bedtime ritual regardless of how many times I have yelled at them that day. Here's what we do: A Connor cuddle, a Griffin Grab and a Casey Kiss, then Bob and I say, at the same time, a 'big hug' and 'a big kiss' and then we say together 'I love you very much'. This happens pretty much every night, so that means it was a good day".

Erin: "A good day is everyone enjoying each other and laughing. Happiness is the sweet little things the boys do like going out of their way to perform an act of kindness for someone else. When I see this, it makes me very happy".

DeniseB: "A good day is when no one pisses me off too badly. Not having people cut me off while I'm driving, having someone just be nice to me, getting a phone call or a card from someone I haven't spoken to in a long time (not you Judy that's my fault)". Note from author. DeniseB is always very prompt at returning my calls!

BethL: "A good day is productive at work, home at a decent hour and dinner with my husband before 9pm. A good day off would be spending it with my husband exploring a part of the US we haven't seen yet. Little things that make me happy are; chocolate, a cool breeze, and the way the air smells after it rains, the sound of the waves crashing the shore at Fenwick Island, DE. The considerate things that my husband does for me, like making dinner and doing the dishes make me happy and grateful".

Tracy: "A good day is when I don't have to scream at my kids! When my house is straightened and the floor is clean. Having one of my kids say 'I love you' or 'you're the best mom ever', or just watching them play".

Jenny: "Who said 'A good day is one where I wake up'? That is true. A good day is one where I don't have on my Pj's bottoms when I get to work. See? Keep your standards low enough and you too can have all good days! Seriously, a good day is one where I feel like I've done my best at everything I've tried, and I've tried to get the most out of it and maybe spent it with family or friends. Many little things make me happy. I'm a simpleton. I love laying in my cozy bed, having a stretch and gradually waking up while I work out, reading a good poem, listening to good music taking a shower. I love my ride to work it's beautiful. I drive from the city to the country and watch the sunrise. I love watching the kids the first time they learn something, or having them hug me in the hall because they are excited to see me. I love talking to friends and family. I love eating. Lots and lots of little things make me happy".

Elena: "A good day at this point in my life is when a day goes by with no stress or confrontations. When the family behaves and I don't feel overwhelmed by all the promises I have made to everyone. Little things that make me happy are when my hair comes out ok or I think I look good in my clothes. I am happy when my husband notices this. I am also happy if I can make someone laugh".

Priscilla: "A good day is when the kids are happy and involved in a good activity (school, sports) and I have a productive day at work helping physicians to help their patients and then we go out to eat at TGIFriday's! Little things like that make me happy. Seeing my kids smiling faces and just having everything go smoothly".

BethR: "A good day is one in which I am busy and productive without being overwhelmed and rushed. It is one in which my children get along and are happy and we even have some time to play. It makes me happy when things go my way, no unexpected stress, maybe having some time to hang out with a friend or even get in an uninterrupted phone call with someone I haven't talked to in a while. And it doesn't hurt if everyone likes what I made for dinner! Or better yet if Joe brings dinner home! See, I am not too tough to please".

Nancy: "I am a very controlling person, and I don't mean that in a bad way. My house has to be clean, organized and everything in its place or I freak out mentally. If I feel my house is in order, the laundry done, the fridge stocked and I still have time to run around with the kids a bit, that is a very good day".

Susan: "A good day for me is when everyone shows up for work, the wait staff gets along with the kitchen staff, and all the equipment is in working order. That is a good day for me at work. Other things that constitute a good day are going down to Long Island to see my nieces and nephews, and getting a nice big hug from them. That's a good day too. The little things that make me happy are coming home from work and hearing on my answering machine 'Hi, it's Chris Panatier, I love you' (you might have to hear it to really understand how cute it is). Hearing from family and friends, a funny story, a nice gesture, a bright sunny day, all those things make me happy"!

DeniseW: "A good day—that is when I wake up on time, after a good 'romp' the night before. The trains and subways run on time, I don't get pushed by anyone in the streets of NY, I have a productive day at work, get home on time, make a nice dinner and get some time to enjoy my husband and daughter".

CHAPTER 30—TELL ME THREE ATTAINABLE GOALS YOU WANT TO ACCOMPLISH IN THIS YOUR 40TH YEAR. THEY MUST BE PERSONAL GOALS, SOMETHING JUST FOR YOU.

Personally I think it is so important to have goals. They can be what keep us motivated, what keeps us going. These goals do not have to be big goals, like running the New York Marathon; they can be smaller like learning how to stencil or do a craft, learn photography or to play tennis. The important thing is that our goals exist, and that we stick to them. Obviously I think it is important to have personal, what some might even call selfish goals. That is why I asked that the 3 goals be just for you and attainable. At this point in our lives I would not consider going for Olympic Gold in Gymnastics to be attainable—taking gymnastics lessons, yes, absolutely. You must be somewhat realistic in your goals or you may be setting yourself up for major disappointment, and who needs that?

The goals we chose were all fairly varied with only one seeming to be a common denominator—exercise, get in shape, however it was termed. Eight of us mentioned this as a top priority. This is a great goal to have because it will hopefully afford us all longer healthier lives, and if it provides a little self confidence and de-stresses us in the process, well, all the better. The remainder of the goals are interesting and fun. Some of them concern serious topics in our lives, such as Jenny's response of wanting to be more financially secure, DeniseB's desire to find a new job and Tracy's goal of starting her own business. I have to admit to loving Tracy's goals. I have heard her mention starting her own business before and I really hope she goes for it. Two of the women list completing their Master's Degrees as a primary goal for the upcoming year. They will be juggling careers, families and going back to school, difficult - yes? Attainable—absolutely—good luck to them. Elena only gave me two goals, but since she is expecting her 5th & 6th children in a few weeks I am going to cut her some slack here. Actually I am going to give her a goal—'keep up the good work'. As far as the more fun or adventurous goals we listed some of them were learning photography, to play chess, teach Yoga and finish decorating our homes. These are all worthwhile and attainable goals. My wish for all of you is that the next time I speak with you, you will be able to tell me how you have attained these goals. Good luck to everyone.

My favorite response is DeniseW's. When asked *"Tell me three attainable goals you want to accomplish in this your 40th year. They must be personal goals, something just for you"*. DeniseW replied: "I want to have a baby. I want to continue to receive accolades at work and I want to have a baby". I have been in her position and I know the amount of determination, faith, luck and sex involved in achieving her goal. I wish her and Alan the best of luck.

Here are the rest of our goals:

Judy: "I could go on and on here, but narrowing it down to three I would say: Get back into shape. I let myself go a little this year, as I was feeling a little sorry for myself when the arthritis first set in. I would like to learn to play Chess, the boys both play and I would like to be able to play with them. I would also like to learn how to play golf better. I have played a few times with Michael and really enjoy it. I also love that we can do it together. Now I don't know exactly how attainable this is, but I am really starting to feel like I want to publish this book. I know, that's four, but I am the author, I have special privileges".

Evie: "1. I want to complete the Yoga Teachers Training course. 2. I want to get involved in teaching Yoga to teenagers. And 3. I want to do some type of volunteer work".

Sophie: "My goals include running 4 miles in 36 minutes (that's not really for me but for work), losing 20 lbs. (I have already lost 5) completing a master's degree in social work and to make time for enjoyable activities despite my hectic schedule and tiredness".

Ellen: "I would like to take photography classes and learn how to take really wonderful pictures. I would like to be able to maintain my size 6-8 (that's the vanity in me) since I had been a size 10 since my late 20s. I like where I am now".

Erin: "Too difficult a question to answer".

DeniseB: "I would like to lose more weight, get a new job and finish decorating my apartment".

BethL: "I want to work toward, if not finish, my masters degree. I would like to earn the Expert Field Medical Badge; it is the hardest badge to earn in the US Army. I would like to become more organized in regards to my personal affairs (bills, finances, home repairs)".

Tracy: "To exercise regularly to eat better and to start my own business".

Jenny: "I would like to work fewer hours than the 60 hours a week I average now. I would like to be in the best physical shape possible and I would also like to feel more financially secure".

Elena: "I would like to lose weight. I would like to increase my self-esteem with regards to my body and body image. I would like to be appreciated and recognized one time for doing something valuable for someone else".

Priscilla: "1. Lose 5 pounds. 2. Take a cruise with my family. 3. Finish decorating my house".

BethR: "I would like to do something with my professional life. I am not sure exactly what, but I am working on it. It would be nice to lose 10 lbs so that I feel a little better about myself and how I look. And it would be nice to spend some more time with my girlfriends, like maybe start one of those girls' weekends, or even just find more time for myself to do creative things like paint".

Nancy: I want to have firm upper arms. I want to find a good electrolysis technician. I want to get back in touch with long lost friends and bring them back into my life".

Susan: "My three attainable goals are: 1. Clear up my credit card debt. Don't get me wrong, I am not out of control, but I do have about $2500-$3000 that I need to take care of. 2. Quit smoking. This is going to be the toughest one. I love smoking and I hate smoking, and it is such a hard habit to break. But then I think of all the money I could be saving, maybe I could be putting that money toward my credit card debt! 3. Drop 10 pounds (is there a woman out there who doesn't want to do this)? I want to turn 40 and look the best I have ever looked".

DeniseW: "I want to have a baby. I want to continue to receive accolades at work and I want to have a baby".

CHAPTER 31—WHAT CHARACTERISTICS DO YOU VALUE IN PEOPLE CLOSE TO YOU? WHAT CHARACTERISTICS REALLY RUB YOU THE WRONG WAY? HAS YOUR CORE GROUP OF FRIENDS CHANGED MUCH IN THE PAST TEN YEARS?

Remember question #16? Remember I promised to try and see if there were any comparisons in the answers to the two questions? Well I remembered! Let me refresh your memory a bit. Question 16 asked how we wanted to be remembered by our family and friends. It was the morbid question, at least according to Evie. Through our responses we learned that in addition to being remembered as good, kind, loving people that there were also a few other qualities we would like our loved ones to have associated with us. We wanted to be remembered as a person you can count on, as an honest person, as a good listener, as a loyal friend, as someone who kept a level head at all times, as someone with a good sense of humor who can even laugh at themselves. So let's check if those characteristics we wanted to attribute to ourselves are the very same characteristics we value in the people closest to us. It seems quite a few of these have indeed been repeated here in question #31. Evie, Sophie, DeniseB, Elena and I all place honesty at the top of our list. A sense of humor is also a good quality to have with several of the girls choosing that as a desirable characteristic. Loyalty, sincerity, integrity, they are all mentioned here, much as they were in question #16. They say (has anyone ever found out exactly who 'they' is)? we tend to like people who are like us. That is unless of course you don't like yourself very much. So it only seems natural that we would value those qualities in others that we value in ourselves. One or two of the more unique responses were from Jenny who adds to the usual list 'a sense of curiosity about the world', and from Ellen who admires humility and someone willing to take an occasional risk. What we really don't like seemed to be an easy enough question. Jealous, petty people, with no regard for other's feelings seemed to top everyone's list. We do not appreciate people who are too full of themselves or impressed by their bank accounts. The word judgmental came up more than once. I don't really think any of us like to be judged, and some people seem to be passing sentence on others all the time. We could all live without this. Two-faced, back stabbing, mean-spirited people definitely make our lists of qualities that just 'rub us the wrong way'. You will have to read on for the rest, and there are many more.

As for our core group of friends…well, many of us, myself, Evie, Jenny, Elena, Priscilla, Ellen, Erin, and Susan have all know each other since college. That may not sound like much, but it is now over 20 years! Ugh! Evie, BethL and I both have a few friends who we grew up with, from the age of about 3 that we are still friendly with. Tracy, BethR and DeniseB are still in contact with their high school friends and their college friends too. What has happened for most of us is that our core group has not changed so much as it has perhaps expanded. We have kept that small group of girls we were so tight with so many years ago and added a few new friends along the way. Personally I find it endearing that so many of us have remained friends with each other for so many years. In a day and age where distance and hectic lifestyles tend to keep people apart it is sure nice to know that you have your girls to lean on.

It's time for the old favorite response. This one was kind of a toss up for me. I had trouble deciding between Elena and BethR answers. Actually they are both pretty similar and perhaps that is what made it so difficult to choose. In the end I have decided to go with BethR. When asked, **"What characteristics do you value in people close to you? What characteristics really rub you the wrong way? Has your core group of friends changed much in the past 10 years"?** BethR responded: "I like people who are fun, energetic and loyal. I like being around people who raise their children with similar values to mine because they are so much easier to hang out with. I really dislike people who are quick to complain and never willing to try and change what they are complaining about. My core group of friends has changed but most due to geography. I am still in contact with many friends from my elementary school (Wilson) high school (South Side) and college (Villanova)".

I think we can all relate at least somewhat to what BethR is saying. It goes back to the fact that we do indeed like people who are like ourselves. Many of us are finding, at our advanced age, that we no longer have any tolerance for negative, whiny people who constantly complain.

Here is what the rest of us value in our family and friends, and what really just pisses us off:

Judy: "I really prefer a 'what you see is what you get' type of person. I value honesty, integrity, loyalty, a good listener and a backbone. What I cannot tolerate are hypocrites, these people bore me to tears. Say one thing, do another, ugh. People who are overly jealous, petty and envious drive me to distraction. They spend half their lives cataloging what everyone else has without taking any time to be thankful for all the wonderful things they have. These people are usually petty and insecure too. My core group of friends has remained the same since elementary school (Tracy was in my kindergarten class) but has expanded over the years. Michael once said that I keep in touch with everyone I ever met".

Evie: "Openness, honesty, sense of humor, trust, caring, generosity of spirit and friendliness. These are the things I value in people. What I dislike are people who are conceited or impressed with themselves, selfishness, people who are judgmental, bigots or someone who is overly impressed with money or looks. Luckily for me my core group of friends has not changed too much. My two closest friends and I have known each other since we were three. We grew up across the street from each other. It is more like having 2 more sisters. I have 8 friends from college, including Judy, Jenny, Ellen and Erin. We have all been friends for over 20 years. We don't get to see each other as much as we used to, but when we do it is as if no time has passed. That is my favorite kind of friend".

Sophie: "Above all other things I value honesty. I also like a sense of humor. What bothers me most is insincerity in other folks. If it seems that someone is acting in a way that is fake or forced I will try and find a way to put some distance between us. I may not feel compelled to call them on it, but I will often check my perceptions with someone I trust just to be sure I am giving them the benefit of the doubt".

Ellen: "I appreciate people who are humble, appreciative of what they have, can let their hair down, are kind, funny, sensitive, outgoing and can throw caution to the wind occasionally. I really dislike people who are judgmental of others, especially parenting skills, place too much value on success and material things, are pretentious, uptight, cynical and mean spirited. I am still close with all my Siena college friends and with my high school friends. No matter the distance or the time spent without chatting, I always feel I can pick up the phone and we will be right where we left off. People change over the years, but I feel that I have been a pretty good judge of character and know whom I am comfortable with. I'm not sure I have a core group of friends right now, I have lots of individual friends and some know one another and some don't. I kind of like it that way".

Erin: "My first thought, after thinking long and hard, was that I value a person's dignity. But what does that really mean? So I looked it up. 'The quality of being worthy of esteem or respect. Nobility of character'. What rubs me the wrong way are people who think they are better than everyone else".

DeniseB: "I value honesty and friendliness in those I am closest with. I really don't like people who are back-stabbers. I don't think my core group has changed much, except that now I am closer with my single friends".

BethL: "I value a sense of humor. I appreciate when people take what they do seriously but don't take themselves too seriously. Although we all do it, I hate whiners! It's ok to vent, but someone who constantly complains about life just gets on my very last nerve. I am still friends with people I have known my whole life. I am lucky to be able to pick up the phone and it is just like I spoke with them the day before. My local friends have changed, but that is due to the life I've chosen in the military. I am more choosey about who I spend my time with. I make sure that they have similar core values and ethics as I do".

Tracy: "I value honesty. I can't stand people who are two-faced. My core group has not really changed, I have sets of friends, high school, college and local friends".

Jenny: "I like kindness, compassion, sensitivity, consideration, a sense of humor, respect for others, open-mindedness and a sense of curiosity about the world. The thing that bothers me more than anything is inconsideration for other, also arrogance, insensitivity and close-mindedness. Oh, and picky eaters. I hate picky eaters! In the past 10 years my group of friends has remained pretty much the same, although I have added some along the way. The biggest change for me has been my move back to Syracuse. I see my friends less and haven't made many friends here yet".

Elena: "What I value in people close to me is honesty, friendship, someone I can confide in and trust, a person who is easy to be with and that shares some of the same values and beliefs as I do. Characteristics that rub me the wrong way are; negativity, I am so sick and tired of hearing only the bad side of things, how everything always goes wrong and how they are never responsible for their own actions".

Priscilla: "A sense of humor, insight into other people's feelings and consistency. I can't stand people who are insecure and unhappy with themselves. They should have it figured out by now. My core group really hasn't changed except that I now have a close friend from work who was not in my life 10 years ago. Many of my college friends still live in the area, as I do, and our kids are growing up together which is awesome".

BethR: "I like people who are fun, energetic and loyal. I like being around people who raise their children with similar values to mine because they are so much easier to hang out with. I really dislike people who are quick to complain and never willing to try and change what they are complaining about. My core group of friends has changed but most due to geography. I am still in contact with many friends from my elementary school (Wilson) high school (South Side) and college (Villanova)".

Nancy: "I value humor, flexibility, understanding and a good heart. I despise people who are back stabbers, judgmental and competitive. My core group of friends are the ones who are most like me; have kids, like to try new things and new places, are spontaneous and flexible".

Susan: "I value people who are real. By that I mean people who don't put on airs about who they are, who they know, what they have, that kind of thing. I value people who are honest and open. I like people who can tell you the truth and don't mind hearing it. We are who we are. Be that person. My core group of friends has not really changed much at all in the last 10 years. I am still as close to all my college girlfriends as ever and still have a few good friends from when I was young. I have made other friends along the way, but my friends from high school and college will be my friends forever".

DeniseW: "I value honesty, loyalty, a happy outlook on life and knowing that I can count on them. I don't like people who are confrontational, egotistical, selfish or judgmental. I don't have any of the same friends I had 10 years ago. I am very glad about that".

CHAPTER 32—HAVE YOU EVER HAD ANY DIFFICULTY TURNING ANY OF THE MILESTONE AGES (IE; 18, 21, 30, 40)? OR ANY AGE FOR THAT MATTER? HOW DID YOU GET OVER IT?

We have in our culture what we call the "milestone ages". They generally end in a zero or a five, for example, 35 and 40, but also include 18 and 21. Don't ask me who decided these numbers should be milestones, but once again I feel confident blaming a man. If you are not sure what a milestone age is, it is simple. A milestone is event, like a birthday, that should be remembered for its importance. There, I made it sound nice. At our milestone ages we are supposed to reflect and take stock of our lives. If we are lucky, we will walk away happy with who and where we are and go on and celebrate our birthday. If we aren't so lucky, well your birthday is pretty much shot to hell. All the birthday cake Carvel can dish out isn't going to make you happy now. Remember, you still have the upper hand here. If you decide things are not the way they should be, or you are not the way you would *like* to be, change. That's what is great about milestones; you can view it as an opportunity to bask in your achievements and happiness, or as a harbinger of change. Either way, you win. For most people turning 18 or 21 means only one thing—legal drinking age, perhaps for those more civic-minded folk, the right to vote. It would appear that these ages are a breeze and that no one would have any difficult turning 18 or 21. In fact many people do, I guess I just didn't interview any of those people, and that kind of surprised me. Eighteen and twenty-one are the beginning of the so-called "adult years". This implies added responsibilities, going to college, choosing a major, finding a job, paying rent and bills, being on your own. At 18 we can actually have a say in who becomes our President! That is a big responsibility. We can go to a bar and order a drink with our own ID. There are a lot of changes going on here. It seems to me that we should be more overwhelmed by turning 18 or 21 than by say, and l am just choosing a number at random here, 40. I think we were all too busy enjoying our newfound freedoms and bar hopping ability to realize we were on the brink of adulthood. What is funny is that several of the girls had trouble turning "non-milestone" ages. BethL and Sophie both had some difficulties with 33. What is interesting is that sometimes it is not so much the number as what is going on in our lives at the time we turn, say thirty-three. BethL and Sophie both mention changes in their lives or lifestyles at that point that may have caused the problems with turning 33. DeniseB on the other hand seems to dislike those ages that end in "9", maybe she is thinking about what comes after "9", maybe she had a bad experience at age 9 and now hates that number? I think she should go see a psychic and find out. I am kidding you do know that right? Tracy, Priscilla and Evie had some difficulty with a more traditional age, the big 30. I think for women, 40 may be the most difficult, but thirty is the second runner up. Evie tells us about feeling like her "30 year warranty" had just expired (and she made me laugh again), for Tracy and Priscilla it was just difficult, but not for any reason that they could put a finger on. The rest of us, at least so we say, have not had any trouble so far turning any age. What is great is that even those ladies who admitted having some trouble turning 30, 33, 39 whatever, still feel that 40 isn't going to be a problem. You have probably have had a chance to get to know "my girls" quite well by now so you feel as confident as I do in saying that they will sail through 40 with a smile of their faces, proud of who they are and what they have achieved. It made me feel good just to write that. I feel good just knowing these women. Right now I am missing them all a lot. It is true in my *old* age I have become a sap.

OK, this is my favorite response. When asked, ***"Did you ever have difficulty turning any of the milestone ages (ie; 18, 21, 40), or any age for that matter? How did you get over it"?*** Tracy responded: "Thirty was hard, but not terrible. I wasn't a kid anymore, you know? Life just goes on and you get used to it. I had a child, a husband and a home. I got over it".

My feeling here is that Tracy did exactly what was expected of her at the milestone age of 30—she was not thrilled with it, she took stock—good husband, family and home, and just got over it. Amen.

Here are the rest of our comments:

Judy: "So far no age has bothered me. Talk to me on December 19, 2002 and we will see if that still holds true. This is the day I turn 40. My friend Karin told me that until then I can 'talk the talk and walk the walk' but on the 19th of December it will be another story. We'll see".

Evie: "Not emotionally, but 30 was tough physically. I had a lot of things go wrong in a short amount of time. I swore my 30-year warranty had expired! The physical limitations did depress me at the time. I just worked really hard at getting better physically and joked about it, and the bad feelings finally passed".

Sophie: "Thirty-three was the most difficult birthday for me and it was just because of the number. I didn't feel any different but that was the year I became aware that my metabolism was slowing down. It now takes longer to lose weight and longer to get back into shape. I didn't really do anything to get past it except just keep on truckin'".

Ellen: "At age 35 I was the mother of 2 small children, had a husband who worked full-time and attended Law School and I was working part-time. I had no family to speak of in the area and I felt the struggle. It felt like, wow, where have all the good times gone"?

Erin: "No, I never gave any age much thought".

DeniseB: "I seem to have difficulty with the year preceding a big one, i.e.; 29, 39".

BethL: "I didn't like turning 33. I think it was more about what was going on in my life than about the number itself. I was changing careers and leaving my boyfriend at the same time. I was scared about being truly on my own for the first time in ages. I decided to take stock of my accomplishments and blessings and not give myself any time for self-pity. That is how I got past it".

Tracy: "Thirty was hard, but not terrible. I wasn't a kid anymore, you know? Life just goes on and you get used to it. I had a child, a husband and a home. I got over it".

Jenny: "No, I have never had any difficulty with my age, so far it has all been fun".

Elena: "Thirty-five was a milestone age for me. I didn't want a big celebration but I also didn't want it ignored. I wound up just letting it go without any fan fare".

Priscilla: "Yes, I have. Twenty-five and thirty weren't great but for some reason 35 was no big deal and 40 doesn't look to be either. I am better off financially than I ever imagined and I love having 'older' kids so I think that my 40's are going to be a lot of fun! During the 40s my children will graduate from high school and college and my 50 will then open up a whole new world for me".

BethR: "No, but I do remember being especially happy to reach 18 and then disappointed to discover that Pennsylvania (went to college at Villanova) had 21 as the legal drinking age. Numbers don't really bother me much, not yet".

Nancy: "Turning 30 was really tough for me for some reason. It's because I felt that I had given up the glamour of New York City for the suburban life and I felt like I was turning into a boxed-in suburban housewife".

Susan: "I have not had any difficulty with any age yet. Forty remains to be seen. Eighteen was the legal drinking age, 21 meant you were an adult and 30 made you feel more mature and established. Thirty-five was just 35. Forty will be the hardest by far".

DeniseW: "My most difficult year was 29. I had moved back in with my mother, I was not in a relationship and I still didn't know what I wanted to do career wise. I sat in the dark and cried for hours. I got over it the next day".

CHAPTER 33—HOW DO YOU PLAN TO CELEBRATE (AND YOU SHALL CELEBRATE) YOUR 40TH BIRTHDAY?

It appears that most of us would like to celebrate this day in one-way or another. I really think it should be celebrated. I hate to say 'look how far we've come' but it is so true. We have so much to celebrate. We are all healthy, except for minor aches and pains (unfortunately commonplace at our age). We have wonderful families, careers and friends. We have so much to look forward to; it almost becomes an issue of 'why wouldn't we celebrate'? I think the subject of whether or not to celebrate is directly related to how you feel about turning 40. The women interviewed in this book are obviously very comfortable with this. It is worth noting that many people are not. I know a few people, remember my friend who spent the day in bed with Haggen Daas, who are dreading it. They are very melancholy and don't even want to talk about it, as if that is going to stop 40 from coming! I really think this is sad, and I feel badly for them, but part of me just wants to smack them and shout 'snap out of it'. Perk up, count your blessings and get over it! For the rest of us, we have some very specific ways we want to spend our 40th. Ellen cracks me up the most here. "'Attention Bob, throw Ellen a party"!!!! This is the second time in the 40 questions that Ellen says she wants a party. This is exactly what she should be doing, saying what she wants. I can't stand women who say 'I don't want a present or a party, blah, blah, blah" when they are secretly hoping that their husbands will throw them a big party, and buy them a 'to die for' gift. So many of these poor husbands believe what their wives are saying, (though you would think they'd get the idea after a few years of this) don't have a party or get together, don't buy a present and then wonder why they don't get any sex for three months. Too many women are afraid, embarrassed or ashamed to ask for what they want. Please don't expect your husband to be a mind reader—they are no good at it, nobody is. Speak up. We all have and here are some of the ways we want to celebrate. Evie, BethL, Elena, Susan and Tracy all want a get together of some kind, not a big deal, family and some friends. I think this is a lovely idea, small and intimate. Just as long as the birthday girl is not responsible for the cooking and cleaning at this gathering! Priscilla has some big plans that I can't wait to hear all about next year!! And our Nancy, boy has she been planning, trips to Italy, cruises, etc…busy lady, can't sit still for a minute, that's our Nancy. I am still not exactly sure how to spend my day, although some sort of Spa treatment will be involved. Jenny and Erin haven't given it too much thought yet—have I taught you nothing girls????? Times a wasting, 40 is less than one year away, get busy. I was happy to hear that everyone wants to do something and that we have no 'crawl in a hole' types here. Once again, I ask you, what *isn't* there to celebrate?

I think for favorite answer I am going to go with Ellen for the reasons I stated above. Here is her response when asked, *"How do you plan to celebrate (and you shall celebrate) your 40th birthday"?* "I plan to have my husband throw me a party. It doesn't have to be on my birthday but at some time during the year. I plan to take a vacation to celebrate being 40 and fabulous and that I have made it with the man of my choice for 10 years! I plan to feel good about hitting maybe the half way mark and will look to the next 40 years to be as rewarding as the first 40".

I like Ellen's response for a few reasons. First and foremost she is asking for exactly what she wants, this is always important when dealing with husbands and birthdays (or any day that involves gifts). So many people are afraid to ask for what they want or need, it just so happens I didn't interview any of them! I also like her response because it is positive and upbeat. She will be celebrating not only the fact that she is fabulous now, but also that fact that she plans on the next 40 years being just as "rewarding" as the previous 40. Good attitude Ellen.

Sophie's response was also truly inspirational and heartwarming but I am going to make you read on to find out what she had to say.

Truthfully as long as we are celebrating, in whatever way makes us happy, that is the important thing. Birthdays should always be celebrated because it means we have lived another year, hopefully a good year. If it was a bad year, that's ok too, because it's OVER! Celebrate the start of a new, better year! The rest of us also had pretty positive attitudes and some fun plans for our 40th birthdays, here they are: Husbands pay careful attention.

Judy: "I plan on milking this for all it's worth! I want a really good gift, no party, spend the money on the gift! I have wanted a mink for over 15 years, but am starting to wonder exactly where I would wear it??? I am not subtle when it comes to what I want, you cannot be subtle with men, you must say what you want and where they need to go to get it. My husband gives excellent gifts so I am not worried. If you are looking for me on my 40 birthday try a Salon and the mall".

Evie: "Well for me it's not happening for a little less than a year. I really don't know what I will be doing, but I know a celebration of some sort will take place. Crawling in a hole is not an option. I don't recommend it as I have been there before. I truly believe it's not the number, it's how you feel".

Sophie:"My 40th birthday was on a Sunday and I stood up in church and told the whole congregation that I praise God for helping me make it to 40. I was as joyful as I could be. I went out to dinner with my family, but was a bit disappointed that they didn't sing 'Happy birthday.'"

Ellen: "I plan to have my husband throw me a party. It doesn't have to be on my birthday but at some time during the year. I plan to take a vacation to celebrate being 40 and fabulous and that I have made it with the man of my choice for 10 years! I plan to feel good about hitting maybe the half way mark and will look to the next 40 years to be as rewarding as the first 40".

Erin: "I don't have any plans yet". Note from author—I will have to be responsible for getting Erin some plans!

DeniseB: "I went out to a bar in NYC with some friends and had a party with my family at my sisters".

BethL: "I hope to spend it with my twin brother Jim, my husband, Richard and my brother's wife Lisa. She is also one of my closest friends and is just one week older than Jim and I. I don't want any presents other than the *presence* of my family, some great food and some frosty, cold beverages. Birthdays are an accomplishment and something to be proud of. If you choose not to share your age that's ok, but always celebrate it. My Grandmother in-law has a saying 'age is a number and mine is not listed'! She is 78 years old, works part-time, travels the globe and goes dancing with her friends. She is another one of my heroes".

Tracy: "I do not want a surprise party but we may just have a party, not necessarily a *birthday* party because I don't like being the center of attention".

Jenny: "Since it is almost a year away I haven't planned anything YET. I don't know what I will do; probably just live a normal day.

Although my birthdays don't bother me I don't usually like to make a big deal out of them".

Elena: "I would prefer a small group of my closest friends to go out to dinner to mark this momentous event. No gifts, no surprises, no hoopla"!

Priscilla: "I am taking a cruise, remember"!

BethR: "I will definitely celebrate turning 40. How I do not know, but please feel free to throw me a big party and send great gifts. It's a long way off to be planning already. Interestingly enough when I was reading through the by-laws of the fire department I discovered that you have to be 40 or under to become a member. I cut that pretty close"!

Nancy: "I plan on taking full advantage of it all year long. I have planned a trip to Italy with my husband for a week, without the kids, and my girlfriends and I are planning a cruise to the Caribbean. I'm sure I will think of more things to do to hide the pain"!

Susan: "First of all I hope I am lucky enough to have the day off! It seems that I am always scheduled to work double shifts on my birthday. I don't know how this keeps happening, but it does. I think I might like a nice dinner out with some of my friends. My birthday is the day before New Year's Eve so maybe I will just celebrate then instead. I have a little over a year to think about it. Who knows, when it finally gets here I may want to crawl in my bed and cry, I hope not, but maybe".

DeniseW: "I kind of answered that in question #1".

CHAPTER 34—LIST THREE ADJECTIVES THAT BEST DESCRIBED YOU THROUGH YOUR TWENTIES AND THIRTIES. OK, NOW LIST THREE ADJECTIVES THAT DESCRIBE YOU NOW. HOW DO FEEL ABOUT THE CHANGE, IF ANY?

I was asked to describe myself in 3 adjectives on a job interview with First Boston several years ago. I do remember listing "assertive and personable" but I honestly don't remember what my third adjective was. It obviously left enough of an impression on me for me to modify the question and include it here. It is one of those questions that make you think about yourself in terms of how you present yourself to others. No one mentioned any physical characteristics like pretty, tall, muscular, toned, thin, the really shallow stuff. And though we have all changed so much in the past 10-20 years we have also not changed much at all. Does that make sense to anyone besides me? I guess what I am getting at here is that our fundamental personalities have not changed. If we were good, kind, loving, and law-abiding people in our twenties, we have not become bad, selfish, havoc reeking criminals in our thirties. For Sophie it was somewhat the opposite, her 20s were not the happiest, most focused time of her life, but with hard work and faith she was able to turn this all around and become the confident, self-assured and yes, happy person we know now. Very important parts of the rest of us have changed too. Some of us, like Jenny, Evie and Ellen miss the spontaneous, wild, fun and carefree people we used to be. It seems that as we age, careers, children, spouses, family responsibility, mortgages, each take away a little bit of these qualities. But I don't believe they are gone entirely. We do wild and fun things; we are just not as *extreme* in our endeavors. Instead of bungee jumping we might instead spend the day at Great Adventure riding the roller coaster or Roaring Rapids (that is wild and fun). It all really depends on how you look at it.

Tracy and Priscilla stuck with the same three adjectives to describe them now as they did in their twenties and thirties, and knowing them, these things haven't changed about them. As I mentioned earlier, our fundamental personalities have not really changed, just a few aspects. The important thing about these changes, as Jenny so eloquently puts it, is that we are happy with the change. If you answered this question on your own and you realize that you are not happy with your 3 adjectives that describe you now, get to work! Hate to quote an old cliché here, but "it's never too late to change".

I am glad we are winding down on the favorite responses. They get more difficult with each question. For this one I will choose…Hmmmmm. DeniseW. When asked: ***"List three adjectives that describe you in your twenties and thirties. Ok, now list three adjectives that describe you now? How do you feel about the change, if any"?*** DeniseW tells us: "In my 20's I think I was happy, a partier and carefree. In my 30's I was fake (tried to be someone I wasn't for the sake of my 1st marriage), unsure and unhappy (the marriage and divorce). Now I am truly happy, secure and confident".

It just seems to me that DeniseW has experienced just about every emotion, the good and the bad. I think she was very truthful here, overcame some bad times, moved on found true happiness and love. Isn't that what it is all about?

We all did a good deal of changing in the past 20 or so years. Here's how we feel we have changed:

Judy: "Let's see, I would say energetic, personable and responsible would pretty much sum me up for the 20's and early 30's. I would have to drop the energetic for sure and I think I could add strong, as in my faith, my convictions and my ability to get through tough situations. I *really* miss the energetic me, but I like the new, stronger version of me too"!

Evie: "Good friend, hard working, partier. Now it would be good Mom, survivor, and good friend. I feel good about the change. I don't miss that 'party' life as much as I thought I would. I still have a good time, and now I actually remember it. Had I known how amazing motherhood would be, I would have stopped being selfish a lot sooner. Hindsight is a great thing".

Sophie: "For the 20-30's I would have to say, unhappy, confused and empathic. For now it would be settled, content and empathetic. I guess I believe these changes are good. I think the part of me willing to sit down and listen to folks has become more refined as I have learned to just listen without having the need to fix everything".

Ellen: "I would go with 'carefree, enthusiastic, and joyful' and now change them to 'enthusiastic, joyful and responsible'. Sometimes I feel resentful about having to think about everything and everyone else. I just want to be able to do things and think about the consequences later, except of course when it comes to my children".

Erin: "Tough question, I can't think of anything".

DeniseB: "Introverted, personable and friendly. I would say that I have not really changed much except that I am less introverted than I used to be".

BethL: "Energetic, gregarious and insecure. And for now I would go with 'confident, caring and dedicated'. I am and will always be a product of my experiences. I am happy about the changes I have made and look forward to changes yet to come".

Tracy: "Honest, caring and thoughtful. I don't think I have changed".

Jenny: "In my 20's I'd say bold, timid and free. In my early 30's I'd say confident, uncertain and fun. Now I'd say confident, brave and calmer. I think I have grown more confident in my ability to take control of my life, but at the same time have become less spontaneous. I guess we all change as we age, it probably wouldn't be a good thing not to. The most important this is that you like the changes you have made, and I do".

Elena: "1. Energetic 2. Fun 3. Focused. Now I would be: 1. Energetic (or trying to be) 2. Focused (though on totally different things) and 3. Reliable. I wish I were more fun. I try and be have a good time with friends but don't always have the time and energy to be 'fun' anymore".

Priscilla: "I would say I was outgoing, fun loving and happy and I guess these will be the same adjective I would chose for now".

BethR: "I really don't think I have undergone any big changes between my 20s and 30's, and now almost 40. I feel like I am still a kid".

Nancy: "In my 20's I was naïve, direction-less and blissful. In my 30's I have been searching, restless and quizzical and in my approaching 40's I am going with harried, happy and appreciative".

Susan: "Young, wild and free. Now I would say not so young, less wild and still free. But seriously, in my 20's and 30's I would say that I was carefree, spontaneous and stress free. I had no obligations to anyone but myself and I lived however I wanted. Now I would say that I was more serious and more responsible, but still somewhat carefree. By this I mean that I am more responsible about my career and my finances, but I still tend to live for myself (since I am single, I can still do this). I never really thought about how I feel about the change. It kind of happens little by little and you don't really notice the changes until someone like Judy asks you".

DeniseW: "In my 20s I think I was happy, a partier and carefree. In my 30s I was fake (tried to be someone I wasn't for the sake of my 1st marriage), unsure and unhappy (the marriage and divorce). Now I am truly happy, secure and confident".

CHAPTER 35—NOW THAT WE ARE 40, IF SOMEONE PAID FOR IT AND IT WAS 100% GUARANTEED SAFE, WOULD YOU CONSIDER PLASTIC SURGERY? WHAT WOULD YOU HAVE DONE?

This seems to be a heated debate with women our age. There are so many options available to us, and so much pressure to look good, that at times it seems more like a 'what' and 'when' issue, not a 'should we' or 'shouldn't we' issue. In recent years alone some non-invasive surgeries have been brought to our attention and are gaining in popularity. The latest of these crazes includes Botox, Lasic (eye surgery). For those of you not in the know, let me do a quick summary. Botox, yes, botox, involves injecting potentially deadly bacteria, that's botchilism, into the wrinkled area that you wish to obliterate. What you get is instant face freeze. Your wrinkles, even the deep ones, will fade almost immediately. One of the side effects reported is that people having the procedure can no longer move their eyebrows and seem to have a "frozen" expression on their face, hence the term "face freeze". However, it should be noted that it is a wrinkle-free "face freeze". This procedure is highly effective but lasts only a short period of time, generally a couple of months. So it will involve life long maintenance. It is fairly inexpensive, in terms of cosmetic surgeries and procedures, running approximately $300-$500 per treatment. It is becoming so widely used that people are having "botox parties" and injecting each other while they socialize. I have a small problem with injecting botchilism into me, but I may be in the minority here. Also common is LASIC eye surgery. This is primarily for those tired of wearing eyeglasses or contacts. LASIC was the choice of BethL who would is frustrated with her glasses and would like to be able to show off her green eyes a bit more. This is a relatively common surgery these days, I myself know 5 people who have had it and all of them came away pleased. LASIC is performed as outpatient surgery, which means there are no hospital stays, and no anesthesia. The surgery is fairly quick, so I have been told by those who have had it, painless and provides almost instant gratification. Of the 5 people I know who had the surgery all claim that within hours their sight improved significantly. No one I know has had any kind of post-surgical problems. This too is affordable, though not cheap, generally running about $5000 for both eyes. So obviously, with this and all the standard surgeries available, one might be inclined to go for it. Let me say, as with any surgery or procedure, there are risks involved and you should weight them CAREFULLY. Make sure all Doctors are board-certified and all technicians are licensed. It helps if you know someone who has had the procedure, whatever it is, done before.

To get right to the point, as a group we would go for it! I think the safety guarantee (that is the only reason I would consider it) and of course the fact that it would be free were the things that put most of us over the edge. It seems that even though we are, in general, a group of self-confident, self assured women we might want to have a little help improving on our God given looks. It is really kind of sad that we feel this way (and I include myself in this). Society, TV, the movies, magazines, everything we see tells us that we are just not quite good enough. We may look good, but we can look better. Jamie-Lee Curtis just did a spread in MORE magazine aimed at this problem specifically. She admits that after years as being held up as an icon of physical 'perfectness' that she submitted to several plastic surgeries. She now feels that she would like to be accepted for the Jamie-Lee she is now, and did an accompanying layout in shorts and workout bra to show how she really appears without any touchups. I thought she looked great. I think she should be enormously proud for taking such a bold step. Most of us will never really have the choice to have plastic surgery because to the masses it is cost prohibitive. But we did feel that there are a few areas that we would touch up, given the ideal circumstances. We decided that our breasts are absolutely too saggy. We don't want bigger breasts, Evie would actually opt for a breast reduction, we just want them back where God intended them to be, you remember, before gravity, pregnancy or breast feeding set in. Our thighs and hips could use a little work, and whose couldn't? Sophie and I went with that one. Erin and Ellen would opt for some facial work and the disappearance of those bothersome wrinkles. There were even a few of us who wouldn't choose any surgery or procedures at all. Man, are they good. Priscilla, Tracy and DeniseB all refused my generous, though make believe, offer. Priscilla was the most adamant and that is probably why I chose her as my favorite response. When asked: ***"Now that you are 40, if someone paid for it, and it was 100% guaranteed safe, would you consider plastic surgery?*** **What would you have done"?** Priscilla adamantly responded: "NO WAY! Ask me again at 50 but I still think my answer will be NO WAY! I like the way I am and I think it looks really tacky when older women try and look too young". I think that is a great answer and I congratulate her for being less vain than the rest of us. However, I do intend to check with her at 50 just to see if she changes her mind.

Here is how the rest of us feel about plastic surgery:

Judy: "Where do I sign up and who is paying? It is the safety part that I need the guarantee on. I always thought that I would want my tummy done (even constant crunches don't help much after 2 C-sections) but now I think I would opt for my inner thighs. I tend to be fairly muscular but this is an area that I can't seem to tone up. I think thinner thighs would give me an overall leaner appearance since I am short, not even 5'2"."

Evie: "The only thing I would ever consider is a breast reduction. They can be a pain in the neck (and back) to carry around! I don't think I'd ever do it though, but if someone was paying for it? Who knows"?

Sophie: "If I ever got plastic surgery, it would be liposuction on my hips, thighs and mid-section. These seem to be the problem areas that I find most difficult to keep in check".

Ellen: "Yes, I would have surgery. I don't like that I can begin to see subtle changes in my features just when I have begun to feel more secure with my body. I would opt for a face-lift and some lipo on my butt. However, only if it is 100% guaranteed that I would not end up looking like a cupie doll"!

Erin: "I would probably go for it. I would like to get rid of some of my wrinkles".

DeniseB: "No, I still wouldn't choose any plastic surgery".

BethL: "WHY NOT? I would have Lasic surgery on my eyes and have my breasts lifted. I am tired of wearing my glasses. My green eyes, so I have been told, are one of my best features. I think I am in pretty good shape (courtesy of Uncle Sam) but gravity has taken its toll on my chest".

Tracy: "No, no plastic surgery for me".

Jenny: "See question #1. No, seriously, I am very ambivalent about plastic surgery. I hate the thought of doing something like that for no other reason than my own vanity, but at the same time, I don't want to end up with little beady black eyes, bags and huge wrinkles. In the end, especially under the given circumstances, I guess I would do it".

Elena: "I never thought I would advocate any kind of plastic surgery, but if it were free and safe I might consider softening one deep wrinkle in my forehead to give me a better chance at keeping my skin looking young. I might also consider liposuction to give me a jump-start on the figure I want and maybe perk up my droopy breasts (from so many pregnancies). I would do this to make myself feel sexy and desirable, not for anyone else".

Priscilla: "NO WAY! Ask me again at 50 but I still think my answer will be NO WAY! I like the way I am and I think it looks really tacky when older women try and look too young".

BethR: "NO WAY. I am a wimp and do just about anything to avoid pain. Besides, what's the point? Who would I be fooling? Is it so other people would say 'boy she looks great'? Or is it so one can lie about their age? If I had a big deformity that caused me to be stared at or that caused people to avoid me I might consider it, otherwise I don't see it happening. Actually I might consider getting my spider veins shot out with saline, but that doesn't hurt. See, I am changing my mind already".

Nancy: "Absolutely, anywhere and everywhere. I would get liposuction on my hips and butt and I would get a breast lift to put them back where they belong"!

Susan: "I don't think that I would ever have plastic surgery, unless I had a disfiguring accident. I can't say that I don't think I need any improvements, because I am certainly not perfect, but I don't think I would do it no matter how safe or cheap. It just isn't me. My only concession to beauty enhancement these days is coloring my hair. If it weren't for those nasty grey hairs that I have had since I was a teenager I wouldn't even bother with that".

DeniseW: "Sure, I would have my eyes done. I hate those wrinkles when you smile. Ugh"!

CHAPTER 36—WHAT PHRASE, CLICHÉ, OR SONG LYRIC BEST SUMS UP YOUR BASIC VIEW ON LIFE?

This is definitely one of my favorite questions, if not my number one favorite. It seems like this simple, little, harmless question, but the responses really reveal a lot about a person and what is going on in their lives at this point. I think I have mentioned earlier that music is such an important part of my life. So many of my memories, good and bad, are tied up in songs. I remember the first song I learned all the words to 'Love and Marriage' by Frank Sinatra (of course). I sat by the 8-track player (ok, so I just dated myself) for hours memorizing the words. I remember my father singing it with me. I remember the first song I ever slow danced with a boy to, it was Earth Angel at the 50s dance at South Side Junior High School. I will leave the boy nameless. I remember playing 'I Will Survive' by Gloria Gaynor over and over each time I was dumped by one of my boyfriends. I remember singing "I Love You Baby" by Frankie Valli and The Four Seasons to my newborn son. I remember most of my friends' wedding songs. Like I said music is important to me, so obviously I went with a song for this question. For me, and I would have to say several of the girls since they too chose song lyrics to sum up their basic view on life, music has a healing power. While music may, "calm the savage beast", for those of who chose song, music seems to have a similar, even cathartic effect. It picks us up, lifts our spirits, and makes us feel good. We actually had what we called the "burn tape" in college. I don't know if any of the girls remember it. This tape was passed around each time one of us was "burned" by a guy (the tape probably disintegrated from overuse). It had songs like "I Will Survive" and "Goodbye To You" by Patti Smyth and Scandal. It really did make you feel better, at least momentarily, I mean who could feel sad when screaming at the top of their lungs "Go on now go, walk out the door, just turn around now, cause you're not welcome anymore. Weren't you the one who tried to break me with goodbye? Did you think I'd crumble? Did you think I'd lay down and die? Oh no not I, I will survive; as long as I know how to love I know I'll stay alive. I've got all my life to live, I've got all my love to give, and I'll survive, I will survive, hey, hey". Of course this has hand motions that go with it, but you will just have to use your imagination. There were lots of songs chosen here, all great, we should make a soundtrack to go with the book. I am going to mention the songs and you can try and figure out which songs go with which lady. Our selections included: Frank Sinatra' s "My Way", James Taylor's "The Secret Of Life" (that one got two votes), Rolling Stones "You Can't Always Get What You Want", The Eagles, "Get Over It", "I Still Haven't Found What I'm Looking For" by U2, 'Morningside' by folk singer John Gorka, and "Girls Just Want To Have Fun" by Cyndi Lauper. See how well you have gotten to know the girls, take a guess?

Not everyone went with song lyrics. Elena chose 2 beautiful, anonymous quotes, both very philosophical in nature, and very deep. Priscilla refers to herself as the 'cup is half-full' girl and she truly is. I believe this to be one of the greatest gifts you can give yourself, a positive attitude. It can change your entire life. I call it a gift you give yourself, because only you can control your actions. We're getting deep here, very deep. Jenny also chose a quote "it ain't over till it's over". Another positive, go get 'em attitude! Never give up; you never know what is waiting around the corner. Or as my favorite character in the world once said "tomorrow *is* another day". (Any takers on that one? I'll bet Jenny knows. I will print the answer at the end of the responses to this question).

I think the combination of quotes and song lyrics say something about all of us. We have all over come obstacles in our life, some big, abuse, infidelity, divorce, insecurity, infertility and some small, attitude, priorities, body image, and we feel all the better for it. We are not a group of women who sit around moping and feeling sorry for ourselves. We move on. We 'Get Over It'. A valuable lesson. Try this someday if you are feeling a bit melancholy, blast, and I mean so loud that the neighbors will begin to wonder if there is a teenager home alone in your house, your favorite song and sing along. Dance if it feels right. Then see how you feel. I bet it's at least a little better.

I must admit to being surprised that Ellen, Tracy and BethR couldn't come up with an answer. I thought this was one of the easy questions. But as we have come to learn, we are all different, what is an easy question for one of us obviously poses a problem for others.

OK, favorite response time. Well, it's copout time again. This is kind of like the question about which actor etc…really floats our boat, all the answers are good, so I am exercising my right not to choose. I hope you like our answers.

Judy: "God, I could go on and on here. My memories are often directly linked to a particular song. Right now I am into Sheryl Crowe's song 'Soak Up The Sun'. The chorus sums up exactly how I feel about life these days. It goes like this 'It's not having what you want; it's wanting what you got. I'm gonna soak up the sun, I'm gonna tell everyone to lighten up. I got no one to blame, every time I feel lame I'm looking up'. I know so many uptight people who could benefit from a good dose of Sheryl! One of my absolute favorites (I want this played at my funeral, how morbid am I now Evie?) is Frank Sinatra' s 'My Way'. I really feel the whole song is true, especially the lyric 'regrets, I've had a few, but then again, too few to mention' and of course 'the record shows I took the blows and did it MY WAY'. I agree with these 100%".

Evie: "Let's go with 'Love Stinks' yeah, yeah!   Just kidding. Actually there is a song that I think really sums up a lot of how I am feeling these days. It is by John Gorka, a folk singer, and it is called 'Morningside'. The words are as follows:

> 'Am I a fool, at this late date
> To heed a voice, that says
> You can be great
> I heard it young now I hear it again
> It says, you can be better than you've ever been
> Don't want to waste what I have to give
> In all of the time that I've left to live
> Don't want to waste what I have to give
> In any of the time that I've got left
> I can do more than I thought I could
> Work brings more luck than knocking on wood
> There's random bad and random good
> Work brings more good luck'

Sophie: "I have often joked about it but the song that sums it up best for me is 'Get over it' by the Eagles, because bad things and good things happen to everyone, the world doesn't owe us anything, and sometimes the best thing to do is 'get over it'. We need to work at what we want".

Ellen: "I don't think I have one".

Erin: "The Secret of Life" by James Taylor. The lyrics are 'the secret of life is enjoying the passage of time'".

DeniseB: "'I Still Haven't Found What I'm Looking For' by U2. The title says it all, and 'Little Bit of Soul'".

BethL: "The Dixie Chicks song 'Wide Open Spaces' The WHOLE SONG is awesome".

Tracy: "Shit happens and then you die" and Maya Anjalou's "You don't know what you know and when you know better, you do better".

Jenny: "'It ain't over till it's over'. The Rolling Stones 'You Can't Always Get What You Want but if you try sometimes, you just might find, you get what you need'. The saying 'you never know a man until you walk two moons in his moccasins'. Right now this whole questionnaire is making me think a lot about James Taylor's song 'The Secret of Life'; is enjoying the passage of time..."

Elena: "There are probably so many quotes that would fit that I can't seem to come up with one perfect one. Here are two anonymous quotes that I am fond of: 'Never drive faster than your guardian angel can fly' and 'what lies behind us and what lies before us are tiny matters compared to what lies within us'". (note: We are pretty sure that the second quote can be attributed to Ralph Waldo Emerson)

Priscilla: "I think I mentioned earlier that I see the cup as 'half-full' rather than 'half-empty'. We all have that choice and isn't it better to be around people who see things in a positive light? I enjoy people who have a positive outlook and are problem solvers instead of people who just sit and bitch and complain their way through life".

BethR: "I can't think of a thing".

Nancy: "The grass is always greener on the other side. I tend to forget how great I have it until I hear about other people's problems".

Susan: "I used to like the song lyric 'I'm young, I'm wild and I'm free, got the magic power of the music in me'. I also like 'Girls Just Want To Have Fun' by Cyndi Lauper".

DeniseW: "Looks Like We Made It, by Barry Manilow".

Looking for the answer to who said, "Tomorrow is another day". It's Scarlett O'Hara Hamilton Kennedy Butler of course, played to perfection by the fabulous Vivien Leigh. My all time favorite movie, in case you were wondering—ooh, that could have been a good "fun" question. "What is your all time favorite movie, why"? Maybe in the sequel!

CHAPTER 37—IS THERE ANYTHING MISSING FROM YOUR LIFE? CAN YOU DO ANYTHING TO CHANGE THIS?

Much to our credit, no one listed materialistic things here. Jenny went for the laugh saying that George Clooney is missing from her life, but not one of us mentioned "things". No one said a summer home, a new car, a trip to Europe, and more money. I think everyone deserves a little credit here. I think people would naturally like to have these things in there life, but there is a difference between something you would like to have that isn't there and something that is *missing*. I'll try to clarify, something you want and don't have can be anything, and I for instance would like to be taller. I want this, I don't have it (height that is) but I don't miss this, I don't long for it, I don't need it and I don't spend much time thinking about it. Is this getting any clearer? Something missing from your life would have to be more along the lines of what Evie said about companionship. It's almost a need more than a desire (to that person of course). A while back I said that each question is open to individual interpretation, this was my interpretation of this particular question and it seems like everyone was right there with me.

I am obviously one of those people who like to ask questions. I think this was something my Uncle Peter started at holidays. At least I remember him and my Aunt Ginny as being the 'question askers". I remember one Christmas the question thrown out was "What was the greatest invention of the 20th century"? We had great answers like penicillin, birth control, the automobile and airplanes. I just remember enjoying sitting around with my parents, cousins, Aunt and Uncle and hearing what everyone had to say. It was interesting, educational and fun, and even the youngest kid could play. And so the seeds were planted. Who knew? My Uncle passed on a few years ago and I hope he is getting a good laugh out of this reference. So what is missing from our lives? Is there anything missing at all? Ellen and Tracy don't seem to think so. They both lead rich, rewarding lives. They are happy with the choices they have made and don't worry about the rest. Good for them. For the remainder of the ladies interviewed there are a few things missing. Evie, who you recall is recently single again after a difficult separation, is missing companionship, and Susan is still searching for her 'dream man'. DeniseB, Susan, BethL and Jenny feel they are missing children and a family, though BethL has plans to achieve this goal one way or another. Let me say, it is always good to have a back up plan, whatever your goals may be. Elena misses the spontaneity that she and Joe once shared, but quite honestly with #5 & 6 on the way, it may be a few years before they are sneaking away on a romantic weekend! These responses are really all changeable, to a certain extent. It is up to the individual to either figure out how to make that change, or learn to live with it if they feel it is truly unchangeable as I have.

The favorite response on this one goes to BethL. When asked the question *"Is there anything missing from your life? Can you do anything to change this"?* BethL answered as follows: "The only thing I haven't done yet is become a mother. If this is to be, ok great, if it is not to be, that's ok too. Richard and I have been discussing adopting a child if we cannot have one naturally".

Guess why I like her answer? She feels there is something missing, she defines it, and she approaches the problem and comes up with a backup plan if plan #1, natural conception fails. I like people with a plan and a back up plan!

Let's see what is missing, or not missing from the rest of our lives:

Judy: "Once again, this goes back to a previous question for me. The only thing missing from my life is a daughter. It is my one big regret in life (as I stated in question 16). Can I do anything about it? Well, I wanted to adopt, but Michael did not. Getting pregnant again is not such a good option for me due to past fertility problems, current ailments and now my age. I think I have pretty much come to terms with not having a daughter, but it hasn't been easy. I just try and concentrate on my boys and all the wonderful things I do have".

Evie: "That's a hard question because my life is very full and really good. Being single after so many years of marriage is a tough adjustment. There are things I like to do, or places I would like to go and I have begun doing a lot alone. That can be really hard but when you do it and get through it, you are that much stronger. I would have to say that companionship is missing from my life right now. Can I change that? Do you know any nice single men? Just joking. I can't say I am looking, but I am getting out and meeting some new people. If I meet someone, that would be great, if not, that will be ok too".

Sophie: "For a long time I thought success was missing from my life. I think it is more about how I was defining success. If success is having the best job, most money and biggest toys, then I am probably not 'successful'. I work hard, love my family and feel content with what I have. I think this is a better measure of success. I guess my point is, look at what you have to be grateful for rather than wishing for what you don't have". Note from author: sounds like Sophie could be a Sheryl Crowe devotee like me!

Ellen: "Absolutely not, I am truly blessed".

Erin: "I miss having more of my family around. I would like for my children to grow up with their cousins. This can't change unless someone decides to move to Virginia! I can't go back to Syracuse, no sun, not ever"!

DeniseB: "A family. I wish I was married and had children. There are things I could do to change this I guess, like get involved in more singles activities, which I do, but not too aggressively. I tend to wait for things to happen to me and sometimes being that way I miss out. I did make a New Year's resolution before turning 40 to be more selfish, which doesn't sound right to some people, but if I am going to meet people I need to get more active. That might mean saying 'no' to some things or some people and I do have difficulty doing that".

BethL: "The only thing I haven't done yet is become a mother. If this is to be, ok great, if it is not to be, that's ok too. Richard and I have been discussing adopting a child if we cannot have one naturally".

Tracy: "I can't think of anything that is missing from my life".

Jenny: "George Clooney is missing from my life! And I don't know what to do about it! Seriously, I think everyone wishes for things they don't have. I don't have a husband or children so that is missing from my life. Am I doing something about it, yes and no. I can only make myself open to things and then see what happens".

Elena: "Sometimes I think there is no spontaneity left in my life. I am not sure I want it added back in though. A surprise weekend trip when Joe and I were dating or newlyweds is one thing. I think with the kids and all I might find it kind of stressful".

Priscilla: "Yes, right now I am missing the passion I once had for my job. I do intend to change this and to find a job that inspires me more. I stay with it now because of flexibility, pay and benefits".

BethR: "No, I can't think of anything missing from my life that would be worth mentioning".

Nancy: "I used to think I needed to have a little girl to complete my life. But I have grown to realize that I don't need that anymore. I can foster my relationship with my boys so that we can be just as close as a mother and daughter. Besides, I don't think I have the energy for a girl and all those raging hormones".

Susan: "Is there anything missing from my life? Yes, I would like to be in a committed relationship with a tall, dark and handsome man! I just want a nice guy. I have not found 'the man of my dreams' yet, so that is definitely something that is missing. On the other hand, I am blessed with a good family and wonderful friends".

DeniseW: "Yes, my sister and father are missing. No I would not do a thing to change it. My father physically and emotionally abused me and my sister played an integral role in trying to have my child taken from me during the custody battles with my ex-husband. She is a very judgmental 'born-again' Christian. Both of these people caused me more strife in my life than they are worth".

CHAPTER 38—HOW IS TODAY'S 40-YEAR-OLD WOMAN DIFFERENT FROM WHEN OUR MOTHERS WERE 40? HOW WILL IT BE DIFFERENT FOR OUR DAUGHTERS?

Someone once said, "the more things change the more they remain the same". I am not sure who said this, but I do believe it to be true. So much has changed since our Moms were forty, it is hard to find a place to start. Women have changed for one. Twenty-five or so years ago when our Moms were forty, the vast majority of women were stay-at-home moms without careers outside the home. Women who did work often did so out of absolute necessity, as my mom did when my Dad died. The occasional woman who did have a career was probably a Teacher or a Nurse. Before you all get your panties in an uproar, I think these are extraordinarily important and demanding professions, the point I am trying to make is that there weren't really many other career *choices* for women at that time. There were very few, if any, corporate CEOs, leaders of industry, Firefighters, or politicians and I don't believe we had any highly ranking women in the military back then. Basically our options, though good ones, were limited. Society also did not cast a positive eye on the woman who worked for what was then called "purely selfish" reasons. Today's 40-year-old woman is just as likely to work outside the home, as she is to stay home. In many cases she even has a choice, full-time, part-time or flextime. She can stay at home for a few years and return to a career outside the home when her children are older (just like Priscilla has). The point is we have more options and more choices that we can make. This is not the only area where things have changed. Jenny and Nancy both mentioned in previous questions that forty used to be perceived as, well, old. This doesn't seem to be true anymore. While forty may not be considered *young*, it is certainly no longer considered old. We don't feel forty and we don't think we look forty, or at least what forty used to mean. We are redefining the word. We are going to give it a positive, sexy, independent, health conscious definition so that people, especially women, can't wait to be Forty.

Many of the girls mention that at forty our Moms had much older children, some of them, like Ellen's mom, had children graduating high school. Sophie is really the only one with children close to this age. Most of us are still dealing with pre-schoolers and elementary age children. Elena remember, is still adding on! This is another thing that most women were not doing when our Moms were forty, having babies! Thanks to amazing advances in fertility treatments women of forty can not only have their fifth and sixth child like Elena (by the way these are natural twins, no chemicals involved), but also can begin their families. With women waiting longer to get married this *option* is essential to us. More changes, more options. And yet there is even more. Today's forty-year-old woman seems to be more independent. We have minds of our own and like to share our opinions, with everyone. We are young, vital and sexy; Nancy says we are more like Heather Locklear. That may be stretching it just a bit, but you get the point. We get out more and do more for ourselves, just think back to question # 21, "tell me 3 things you do just for you". Do any of you ever recall your Moms going away for a long weekend with her girlfriends? I certainly do not! Perhaps we feel more comfortable discussing formerly "taboo" subjects with our children. We are probably a little more open about sex. All of us have had to have discussions with our young children on abductions, improper touching and drugs. I don't think our Mother's worried much about these things at all, or at least until we were much older, and then their biggest fear was probably that we would get, hold your breath, *preggers!* This almost seems like a paltry fear (and so easy to prevent these days) when compared to abduction, drug addiction and molestation. Elena addresses the safety issue, talking about not being able to send her children out on their bikes for the day like she did when she was little. She feels that we are consumed with our children's safety. An issue our Moms really didn't have to deal with. Back in our Mom's day family usually lived close by. This is not really the case anymore. People seem to be scattered all over the map, as we the children move for job opportunities and our parents fly away to warmer climates for health and financial reasons. I personally miss having my family close by. Erin also mentioned this in a previous question. When my Mom was my age her sister and mother lived in the same town. My Dad's brother and his family lived 15 minutes away. I grew up seeing my cousins on a regular basis and I loved that. We don't really have that now; most of the family is at least an hour or more away. I miss this tremendously. I miss it for me and for my children.

Yet so much has remained the same. Moms still love their kids. We kiss their wounds, read them stories, chauffer them all over town, hug and kiss them (even when they beg us not to), tell them how great they are, cheer their wins and help them deal with their losses. We put them first, right where they should be.

My favorite response was Jenny's. When asked *"How is today's 40-year old woman different from when our Mother's were 40? How will it be different for our daughters"?* Jenny responded: "There is a world of difference. Forty was old back then! Really old. Now 40 is young. Our Moms were very limited in the things they could do and the way the world thought about them and how they thought about themselves. It will be different for our daughters because they will have even more opportunities than we have had, and fewer restraints".

I just believe everything Jenny said is 100% true.

Here are the rest of our thoughts:

Judy: "I think things are very different today than say 20 or so years ago, especially in regards to my own mother. My mom was a widow at 37 and went back to work full-time to support my brother and I. I am in a much more comfortable situation. When our Moms were 40 there were not as many options for women. Most Moms did not work outside the home; their families tended to live in closer proximity, their children were probably older. I think our mothers were much more into the 'martyr' syndrome of parenthood, I don't think they gave too much consideration to their own needs as women. I think my generation is a bit more self-actualized (in many respects thanks to the women who came before us and showed us the way)".

Evie: "I think and hope that we are more open with our children about subjects that were taboo and therefore not discussed then. The world has changed a lot since we were kids and I hope that we, as women and moms, can keep up and be open to the changes. I can't even imagine how it will be for Cecelia".

Sophie: "My mom and her friends seemed to be focused on being grown-up and composed. I think that 40-year-old women today are freer to speak our minds and do what they want. I think we learned how to trust ourselves. My daughter is already learning to trust her own judgment and bouncing her opinions off of me and off of her friends. She is obviously not grown yet, but she is more verbal and stands up for herself more than I did at her age".

Ellen: "Times have changed so much. Or moms began most of their parenting in their twenties and weren't really encouraged or pressured to work outside the home until it became a financial necessity to pay for college. At least that is how it was in my family. But the time my mom was 40, I was graduating from high school. On the other hand I will have a 2 year old when I turn 40. That seems so strange to me. I think because we were encouraged to achieve more and got married later that we had the opportunity to bring more of a variety of experience to our marriages and our children. However, I do believe there was some sort of contentment for these women at age 40, just knowing that the majority of their child rearing was behind them. Let's face it, raising small children is hard work and we all still have a lot of it ahead of us".

Erin: "I don't really think it is that different. There were great 40-year-old women 40 years ago, and there are great 40-year olds today, and there will be more great 40-year olds in 40 years! It just really depends on the person".

DeniseB: "I think that our mother's generation thought pretty much the same as we do".

BethL: "Most of our mothers didn't work throughout our childhood. It they worked at all it was to help pay for college tuitions or to do something once the kids were out of the house. Many of today's mothers have had to juggle both home and career. They have made sacrifices in not seeing their children grow up. I think today's moms wants to be more of a 'friend' to their children than be an authority figure. This is good and bad, children need their structure and discipline as much as they need love. I hope to benefit from others' experiences and attempt to balance. I believe our sons and daughters will see parents as an entity rather than as separate mother and father. They will have to have role models that are not necessarily gender-related. Relating to the same sex will always be the same, but roles have changed".

Tracy: "I think we are given more opportunities to be who we are instead of what society thinks we should be at 40. I think when my Mom was 40 her children were much older than mine are now, which gave her some more freedom that I don't have yet. I think our daughters will be similar to us".

BethR: "I think it is much different for Moms today. More Moms are working, especially as their kids are getting older. I know that most Moms feel like taxi drivers. There is this need to involve our kids in everything, so they don't miss anything (except maybe playing). This causes the whole family to be in constant motion. You never hear of kids just going out to play or to ride their bikes with a parent. It just isn't safe. Dads are working longer hours than ever. I don't know anyone who works '9-5' anymore like my Dad used to, and because of this most of the parenting and home management falls to the Mom, even if they too are working. I do wonder how it will be for the next generation. I can't see things getting even more crazy, maybe they will be smart and slow things down a bit".

Jenny: "There is a world of difference. Forty was old back then! Really old. Now 40 is young. Our Moms were very limited in the things they could do and the way the world thought about them and how they thought about themselves. It will be different for our daughters because they will have even more opportunities than we have had, and fewer restraints".

Elena: "I think when our moms were 40 most of them were finishing up with regards to child rearing. The kids were older and heading out because they had them when they were younger. I think they were also a little less worried and overwhelmed by their children. Today we are consumed with our children's safety. Our parents wanted us to be safe but did not have to worry about us riding our bikes around the block or going to the playground without an adult. Today I think a 40-year old parent is also consumed with their children's schedules. Too many activities, that begin too young are becoming too stressful for everyone. For our daughters, life will be very different when they turn 40. I see many young women planning careers that they will work at for so many years before they even consider having a family. When they make this decision in their late 30's it will be difficult for them to either stay home or focus on a career. I think there will be a lot of 40 year olds who are feeling unfulfilled because you work so hard to become someone, that you feel you give up a piece of your identity if you stay home to be a mom".

Priscilla: "My Mom always worked as a teacher so I never experienced the stereotype "stay-at-home Mom". I hope my daughter has a choice and doesn't have to work when her children are young if she doesn't want to. I feel that is a difficult time for young mothers.

Once the kids are in school you can work without the guilt because they are doing what they should be and you can too".

Nancy: "Maybe I am biased, but back in my Mom's day, forty was ancient and the women looked the part! Today's 40-year old looks more like Heather Locklear (I know, I'm dreaming) but I think we do look much younger and are more fit than the 40-year olds of yesterday".

Susan: "I think my Mom was pretty cool when she was 40. My Mom was 23 years old when I was born, so when I went to college she was only 41, so I don't see too much of a difference here. Some of my friends had older parents who were maybe a bit more conservative, or stricter than my folks. I would like to think I would be a cool, understanding type Mom. I think we all like to think that our parents didn't understand what it was like to be young, but they actually went through a lot of the same things that we did. Our kids will think we are old and un-cool and don't remember what it is like to be young. We do remember, we've been there and done that, and 'if we leave now we can be in Oswego in 2 hours'"!!!!! Note to reader: This is something that Elena, Priscilla, Susan and I used to shout on the dance floor at 2 am (after several drinks). Occasionally we would actually *leave for Oswego* directly from the dance floor. See, Oswego had an incredibly FUN Rugby team!

DeniseW: "To me, today's 40-year old has more in common with yesterdays 30-year old. When my Mom was 40 I was 20. I am now 41 and my daughter, Sierra, is 6. I think that keeps me young as well. For my daughter I believe that forty will be even younger still."

CHAPTER 39—IS TURNING 40 EASIER FOR MEN? WHY OR WHY NOT?

This is another question that I was sure everyone would agree with me and feel that turning 40 is absolutely, positively easier for men. Well, I was wrong again. I don't actually mind being wrong, especially if it makes for more of a diversity of responses and therefore, more interesting reading. I'm just surprised, that's all. Let's address those of us who feel that turning 40 is easier for men. We had many reasons to back up our choice. One reason is that we feel that men seem to place a greater importance on their careers and what they have achieved in the business world. By the ripe old age of 40, many men have been able to achieve a certain level of success and feel comfortable with that. Men don't seem to have that 'biological clock' ticking, constantly reminding them that their fertile years are running out. As BethL points out, men can be fathers well into their 70's (anyone remember Tony Randall)? They are also considered a major 'catch' if they are single and 40. That's all they have to be. A single 40-year-old woman has to be *fabulous!* A big point was made for the fact that men seem to become more distinguished with age; even grey hair looks good on them! Elena, Susan, Tracy, Nancy and I are really bugged by this, and I kind of think we all are. I mean here we are killing ourselves with exercise, eating right, coloring our hair, moisturizing and more moisturizing, manicures and pedicures, and our husbands roll out of bed and shave and they look good. That is not fair. We ladies have a big axe to grind here. They don't go through menopause, and personally I think that alone makes it harder on us women. I mean seriously, who needs all those hot flashes, mood swings, sleepless nights and aches and pains. We have had to deal with periods our whole freaking' lives, most of us went through pregnancies, labor and delivery more than once (and Elena is helping fill the gap for those of us who haven't done so yet), and now we have to deal with menopause? God is *so* definitely a man. I think men should step up to the plate and take menopause off our hands. We deserve a break! But as I pointed out earlier, not everyone agrees with us. Ellen, Evie and Sophie think that turning 40 just poses different issues for men, and that they deal with it differently. They agree that men tend to spend more time worrying about where they are on their career path, and this may cause them anxiety about turning 40. Erin and DeniseB give them credit and feel that men are dealing with issues about turning 40 just as we are. Jenny and BethR say that the men they know are absolutely having problems turning 40. BethR says some of the men she knows are even worse than the women, getting all cranky and sensitive. Jenny says that some of her male friends had trouble turning thirty, and if this is any indication, they will all have more trouble with the big 40. So we are pretty divided here. Priscilla and DeniseW are not even sure if men have issues; see they both have younger husbands!

That old favorite response time is rearing its ugly little head. Who knew this would be so hard. Only one more to go after this! For this question I think I will choose Sophie. When asked, *"Is turning 40 easier for men? Why or why not"?* Sophie responded: "I don't think that turning 40 is any easier, or more difficult for men. I think their focus is more likely to be on where they are career wise. The physical aspects of turning 40 are less stressful for some men because our culture tends to be more accepting of a man with a little grey hair, calling him mature, than of a woman saying she looks old".

Sophie feels that men just have different issues, but are dealing with major life changes just as we are.

Is turning 40 easier for men? Read these responses and decide for yourself:

Judy: "I think everything is easier for men. They don't have a 'biological clock' or even a 'marriage clock' for that matter. A single 40-year-old man is considered "a catch". I don't think society puts the same label on a single 40-year-old woman. There are far less 'glass ceilings' for men. They are not in constant turmoil over whether to stay home or raise the kids. Their role is pretty well defined. They do not battle with constantly fluctuating hormones and mood swings. There is no 'male menopause', and they get called 'distinguished' when they turn grey! Yeah, it's easier for men".

Evie: "I don't know if it is easier, but I'm sure it's different. I think they value their accomplishments and careers a little more than women do. If that's all in place when they reach 40, then I don't think most men find it difficult".

Sophie: "I don't think that turning 40 is any easier, or more difficult for men. I think their focus is more likely to be on where they are career wise. The physical aspects of turning 40 are less stressful for some men because our culture tends to be more accepting of a man with a little grey hair, calling him mature, than of a woman saying she looks old".

Ellen: "I would have to believe it would be just as much of a turning point for men as it is for women, but for entirely different reasons. The vast majority of men seem to place less importance on the physical aspects of turning 40 (just take a look at the men at your 20-year high school reunion). I feel men place a greater importance on where they are in their careers and how they are doing financially. Although I sincerely doubt they would ever admit to this. How old they are in regard to their children's ages doesn't seem to be a big deal for them either. So yes, I would say if turning 40 were to bring thoughts of where you have been and where you are going, to mind, it would be about the same".

Erin: "No, men have their issues too. Some handle it really well, just like we are and others don't".

DeniseB: "I think that a man turning 40 thinks of the same issues as we do".

BethL: "Yes, it's easier for men. They gain wisdom and respect. They are allowed to have wrinkles and grey hair. They don't go through menopause and can have children up until almost any age! If they had to live our lives they would all be hiding in a closet".

Tracy: "Yes. I don't think they come with the same baggage that we women do. They turn grey and people call them distinguished, we look old. Men fill out, women get fat. I think women in general have to work a lot harder at looking good as we age. I also don't think men get hung up on birthdays and numbers. It is just another year to them".

Jenny: "Not if thirty was any indication! Every guy I know had a harder time turning 30 than any of the women I know. I don't know what it is, other than the fear of death (Mrs. Casterini was right). We'll see what 40 is like for the guys".

Elena: "It seems for most men that turning 40 is not big deal. Most of them even seem to look better. They grow more distinguished and handsome with age. They are also not usually the ones who look back and re-evaluate every decision they have ever made. This is just my opinion".

Priscilla: "I don't really know, my husband just turned 38 and shows no signs of a mid-life struggle".

BethR: "I used to think that turning 40 would be much easier for men, they don't have the whole 'documented' change of life and loss of fertility that we women do. Although it wasn't a big deal for my husband, Joe, I am finding that more of our male friends are struggling with turning 40 than our female friends. The men get so cranky and sensitive about it".

Nancy: "Turning 40 is much easier for men. They get more distinguished looking, more established in their careers and more relaxed about themselves. It seems to be just the opposite for women".

Susan: "Not being a man I cannot say for sure if turning 40 is in fact easier, but I have to think it is. Men get 'distinguished'. Women get older, at least that is the prevailing sentiment. It isn't uncommon to see older men with younger women, and no one thinks much about it when they do. However, an *older woman* with a *younger man* is fodder for much gossip and speculation".

DeniseW: "I truly do not know, maybe not. There's a lot of pressure on men to be 'somebody' by the age of 40."

CHAPTER 40—WHAT DO YOU HOPE THE NEXT 10 YEARS WILL BRING?

Can I have a drum roll please? Part of me never really believed we would get to question # 40, but here we are. What can you say, what does every woman want? A pair of jeans that fit well at a good price! Basically, we all want to be happy. Happiness was the feeling of choice. We all have different ideas of what will make us happy, but in the end this is what we desire most. Some of us chose good health as our path to happiness, not only for ourselves, but also for our children and families. If we are healthy we can work on being happy. Others, like Erin and Jenny for example have a much bigger undertaking, "peace on earth". Wouldn't that be nice? It would be great to live in a peaceful, loving world in which we all co-exist, respecting one another's differences, and even appreciating them. A world where our children are safe to ride their bikes in the street and play outside without the constant watchful, worried eye of an adult. To live in a world where schools are a haven for learning and growing, and not a place where children carry knives and guns. To grow up in a world where children can just enjoy being children. We all hope that the next 10 years will bring us the joy of watching our children grow and prosper. We hope we have done our job of parenting well and that they are becoming good people and caring members of society. Priscilla hopes Ashleigh and Parker will be smart and get college scholarships. I think that is cute! We hope to remember our blessings, and if you have read the previous 39 questions, you know we have many. We want to slow down and "stop and smell the roses" so to speak. We don't ever want to take our husbands and children for granted, even though we probably will. We want to surround ourselves with our families and the friends that we have grown to love over the years. We hope the next ten years will bring us 'much of the same' as BethR so simply puts it. We hope we continue striving to be the good wives, mothers, daughters, friends and employees that we all hope we already are. We hope to be better too, because we all realize that no one is perfect and we can all use a little work here and there. We hope to have more laughter than tears, more love than loss, more good times than bad. More happiness. To me this sounds like the next 10 years are going to be full and exciting for all of us. We have our children to raise, our careers to continue or restart (Tracy, get moving on your business), our husbands to love, or maybe for Jenny, Susan and DeniseB, love to find. We have memories to make, and once Ellen becomes a great photographer she can capture all our memories in fabulous pictures! Who knows what really lies ahead for all of us? I hope we all try and achieve our goals. They are actually in print now ladies, so you're under a little pressure here, and you know me, I will call and harass you about them, because that is what I do! What we do know is that we are one blessed, lucky, group of fabulous women. I hope the next 10 years will bring us all what we are looking for, but more importantly what we need.

Since this is the last question, I am copping out for the last time and choosing everyone as my favorite response. Here is what we all said when asked: ***"What do you hope the next 10 years will bring"?***

Judy: "Health, health and more good health. The rest will fall into place. I of course want happiness, but I feel that is up to me, at least to a certain degree. If you are in good health you can work on providing a good, loving, happy home life for yourself and your family, and if you have all these things what else really matters"?

Evie: "I hope to continue working each day at being a good person. I hope to stay strong. I hope to be a good mother and good friend to my daughter, Cecilia. I hope to be happy more than sad. I hope that I can look at 50 with optimism".

Sophie: "In the next 10 years I hope to see my son and daughter off to college and into their careers. I hope they will start their own families in their late 20s so that I can visit them. I will be retired and I would like to own an RV and travel. I would also like to get licensed so I can work with people in a mental health care environment and assist them in improving their quality of life by teaching them the skills they need to survive".

Ellen: "Excellent health so I can enjoy my children, my family and my friends. Patience in the world. I would like to be a better photographer and find some time to return to the carefree feelings I experienced when I was younger. Since my kids will still be pretty young, maybe I will save that one for the next 20 years".

Erin: "Happiness and Peace".

DeniseB: "Happiness for me and my family".

BethL "I will continue to work hard at my marriage and hope I never take it for granted. I would like to see my family more. I am hoping for two things in the next 10 years. I hope to be blessed with children and they will become my new full-time and all time greatest career. If children are not in my future, then I look forward to a wonderful career as the best US Army officer I can be. I will continue to pray for tolerance and peace in the world".

Tracy: "I hope in the next 10 years I will watch my children grow and prosper. I hope that these years will bring me much laughter and little sorrow. I am hoping to start my own business and would like to be successful at it. I hope my husband continues to be successful in his career and that we are able to do all the things we hope to".

Jenny: "Peace on earth, good will to all".

Elena: "I hope during the next 10 years that I will be able to look at myself and feel good about how I look, act and feel. I hope I will be able to resume my teaching career at some point. I hope to continue providing a good home and loving atmosphere for my family".

Priscilla: "Healthy, smart children who get college scholarships, a job that I love and our mortgage paid off! That way, I will have the 50s until whenever to enjoy my children, grandchildren and live on Cape Cod".

BethR: "More of the same, I hope".

Nancy: "I hope that in the next 10 years I will learn to relax more and learn to really look around at all the wonderful things in my life. I want to take a breath and truly enjoy my life and my blessings. This is the time to enjoy the fruits of our labors".

Susan: "I hope that the next 10 years will find my life a bit more settled. I hope to find that relationship I mentioned earlier (with my dream man) and to have a few children. I would like to spend more time with my family and friends, and less time stressing out about my job. I would also like to feel more financially secure".

DeniseW: "Health, happiness, love, wonderful memories and a wonderful future".

ABOUT THE AUTHOR

Judy Langford, the now 40-year-old author, wanted to write a book for women about women and by a woman. The 40 Questions is her first foray into non-fiction. She has previously published poems in Tomorrow Dream, The National Library of Poetry, and is working on a children's book. Raised in Rockville Centre, N.Y., Judy nurtured a love of writing that culminated in a BA/English from Siena College, and followed with jobs on Madison Ave. and Wall St.

Married since 1988 to Michael, and raising sons Tommy and Danny in New Jersey, Judy hopes the 40 Questions will empower women of all ages with the self-confidence, grace and wisdom that come with age.

www.ingramcontent.com/pod-product-compliance
Lightning Source LLC
Chambersburg PA
CBHW022243290526
45785CB00015B/132